After Pandemic, After Modernity

Other Books of Interest from St. Augustine's Press

After Pandemic, After Modernity
The Relational Revolution
GIULIO MASPERO

ST. AUGUSTINE'S PRESS

South Bend, Indiana

Library of Congress Control Number: 2022938948

Paperback ISBN: 978-1-58731-006-5
Ebook ISBN: 978-1-58731-007-2

∞ The paper used in this publication meets the minimum requirements of the American National Standard for Information Sciences – Permanence of Paper for Printed Materials, ANSI Z39.48-1984.

St. Augustine's Press
www.staugustine.net

Table of Contents

1. Introduction: The Question

A few years ago, I attended the *lectio magistralis* of a colleague who was about to become a professor emeritus and retraced his career, revealing the tricks of his trade and his pedagogical method. This consisted in producing, first of all, chaos in the minds of his students, in order to create space for a reorganization of their mental map of reality. The confession aroused the hilarity of the audience, but I was very impressed, because before moving to theology I worked as a physicist, devoting my doctorate precisely to chaos and complexity. That havoc sown in the cognitive territory of one's students is in truth profoundly healthy and is what teaching conceived as an introduction to reality can and must produce.

Today we escape open questions because we are immersed in a culture of performance. Any inquiry has value only to the extent that it can lead to a solution to a predetermined problem. The only question that is allowed is "how-to?". And the answer is searched for on the internet. A doctor hung a notice in his waiting room: "For those who need a second opinion after Googling, please turn to Yahoo and give way to other patients." The irony appealed to the fact that by now on a mass level we are trying to cure ourselves, to save ourselves. It's all about knowing how to do it, finding the right tutorial. Instead, education and training are based on other kinds of questions: not those that seek a result from an idea we already have in mind, but questions that break through the fabric of our ideas and create space for greater desires and, therefore, for a new, deeper relationship with reality.

This episode in my academic life reminded me of reading

Yuval Noah Harari, an extremely interesting author, also recommended by Bill Gates, who wrote in 2016: "Yet at the dawn of the third millennium, humanity wakes up to an amazing realisation. Most people rarely think about it, but in the last few decades we have managed to rein in famine, plague and war. Of course, these problems have not been completely solved, but they have been transformed from incomprehensible and uncontrollable forces of nature into manageable challenges. We don't need to pray to any god or saint to rescue us from them. We know quite well what needs to be done in order to prevent famine, plague and war– and we usually succeed in doing it."[1] Reading these words after the pandemic caused by Covid-19 can have a tragicomic effect. Certainly medical science has proved extremely valuable, and research into vaccines and their production is playing a key role in this globalised world where not only fashions and musical hits, but also diseases are shared at extraordinary speed.

At the same time, one cannot help but consider Harari's text naive in the light of what has happened: a plague came and a war followed. In a way, the pandemic has produced in us, the world over, a bewilderment and a crisis in the views and certainties we had. That is why I was reminded of the pedagogical method of my colleague emeritus and the idea that in this situation there is also a great opportunity.

In discovering the virtualities of the present situation, I was greatly helped by the sociological analysis of Pierpaolo Donati, an author who over the years has developed a relational framework that has enabled him to investigate in depth what the family is.[2]

---

1   Y.N. Harari, *Homo Deus: A Brief History of Tomorrow* (New York: Random House, 2016), p 1.
2   See P. Donati, *Relational Sociology: A New Paradigm for the Social Sciences* (London: Routledge, 2010) and P. Donati – M.S. Archer, *The Relational Subject* (Cambridge: Cambridge University Press, 2015).

The family, in fact, cannot be considered just a collection of individuals, nor the sum of them, but the sociological study of its role has led this scholar to recognise that relationships have a special reality, which makes the family and society in general irreducible both to the whole and to individuals.

Now, the pandemic has brought relationships to the forefront, first at a physiological level, because the contagion passed right through them, but then, more profoundly, at a psychological and spiritual level. This is where the great opportunity opens up, which this small volume seeks to propose from the perspective of a Christian reading of the world and history.

In fact, Donati's sociological analysis turns out to be really valuable, because it allows us to recognise the relationship as an emergent effect, i.e. as a reality that is brought about by those who are linked but at the same time is greater than them. Just as the relationship of a man and a woman can generate a child, which resembles each of them but has a life beyond them, so in every friendship, in every association, in every significant element of social life a similar phenomenon is at work. The relationship, in fact, at the same time unites and distinguishes those who are in relation, through a double effect that is called by Donati in Latin *religo* and *refero*: The first indicates the element that unites and identifies, while the second indicates the difference and the referral to the other and, therefore, to the beyond, with respect to the subject. And it is precisely this point where the pandemic has revealed the crisis of modernity.[3]

From this perspective, we can say that the virus has functioned as a catalyst for this crisis, highlighting the relational ambivalence inherent in the transition to post-modernity. This provocation allows us to flush out the temptation to simply and lazily fall back

---

3   Cf. P. Donati, *Transcending Modernity with Relational Thinking* (London: Routledge, 2021).

into the pre-crisis comfort zone, without reflecting on the intense phenomena and enduring consequences of what happened. The proposed path culminates with a reference to the cultural matrix and framework as the key to interpreting sociological reality, a matrix that favors or inhibits relational reflexivity. The absence of authentic personal relationships highlighted by the health crisis exposes the consequences of the modern matrix, which, having lost its Christian roots, now risks transforming itself into a digital matrix, substantially configuring itself as a technognosis. What is at stake is our humanity.

This is why we need theology and spirituality. If Pierpaolo Donati is right, in fact, the game is not primarily technological and health-related, but anthropological, philosophical and, therefore, theological. The proposal put forward here is that the loss of the Trinitarian cultural matrix has opened up space for ancient and new idols. But this process, in its very negativity, reveals the greatness of the human being, who is a finite being, but constantly stretched towards the infinite. Even with the transformation of the myth of endless progress into the post-human project, which also inspires Harari, the human being cannot help but affirm his or her humanity, that is, his or her having been created in the image and likeness of the one and triune God. Paradoxically, in seeking to surpass himself, man shows himself to be the image of God. But, without a relationship with the God of Jesus Christ, this tension proves destructive, turning into idolatry.

The path proposed in this small book can be ideally divided into two parts. Chapters 2 to 6 present the pandemic as a great opportunity to recognise the implicit matrices in our culture. Starting from the biblical image of the desert (chapter 2), it will be shown how human beings have historically always run the risk of following a dialectical cultural matrix, as the myths of the ancient regions also reveal (chapter 3). This will allow us to appreciate the relational novelty of the cultural matrix proposed by the Judeo-Christian tradition (chapter 4). In the light of these first steps, it will be possible to illustrate how the tension between human finitude and the desire for the infinite that dwells in the heart of every human being tends to be resolved through the creation of idols which, however, deprive freedom and dehumanise (chapter 5). The pandemic and the clash with limits that followed can then be reread as an opportunity to overcome the idols created both by modernity and by a certain form of post-modernity (chapter 6). This evaluation will lead to the second, applied part of this small volume (chapters 7–10).

Here it will be shown how the pandemic can be read as a discontinuity that introduces a new post-modern epoch not simply because it aims to develop in an even more radical way the attempts of modernity, but because it questions one of its fundamental premises, that is, the dialectic with respect to the religious phenomenon (chapter 7). This, in fact, is inescapable, so that the desert of the pandemic has cleansed certain cultural elements that marked socio-economic life in an idolatrous sense (chapter 8). This step opens up concrete proposals for reconstruction, first of all highlighting the need for a Trinitarian spirituality inspired by the Judeo-Christian matrix which, independently of the religious choices of each person, favours the care of relationships at a socio-political level (chapter 9). But this transformation can only be made possible by an awareness of the role of the universities, which are today heavily undermined by pragmatic and functionalist reductionism (chapter 10). The whole path aims to show the urgency and significance of the final appeal for a real relational revolution in all the (inseparable) spheres of cultural, social and political life.[4]

---

4   The author is particularly grateful for the profound and beautiful discussions with Pierpaolo Donati, a constant stimulus to rethink the data offered by relational sociology from a philosophical and theological perspective. The dialogues with John Milbank, Martin Schlag and Brian Griffiths were also greatly valuable.

The title of this little book intentionally recalls Alasdair MacIntyre's book *After Virtue*,[5] because in some ways it shares the critique of modernity present in that fundamental text and the call for realism. At the same time, the provocation put forward here is not limited to the ethical level, but wishes to provoke a question and critical thought on the whole, the relational rebirth of a Christian humanism, which can make it possible for us to continue our journey in post-modernity without ceasing to be human.

5   A. MacIntyre, *After Virtue: A Study in Moral Theory* (Notre Dame: University of Notre Dame Press, 1981).

2. The Beauty of the Desert

In Europe, the awareness of the seriousness of the consequences of what the epidemic was causing and of the concrete possibility of lock-down practically coincided with Ash Wednesday and the beginning of "Lent", in Latin "quadraginta".

This leads in a spontaneous and natural way to recognize the etymological affinity of this term with "quarantine". The forty years of the people of Israel in the desert and then the forty days of Jesus in the same "place" became like a symbol and a guide in the period of isolation. The question from which the present reflection moves is: Why did God bring His people out of Egypt into the desert, and why did the Spirit lead Jesus there to be tested? What happens in the desert? What can be done where there is nothing, not even the minimum to ensure life? What provision can be made where there is no society? The question is fundamental because one does not end up there by chance or mistake. It is the very Creator who leads to that "place" not only the people, but also His Son who became incarnate.

Theology seeks the answers to questions about the human being and the world by exploring the relationship between reality and the Word of God. From such a perspective, the Book of Hosea offers some indications that may be useful in a first approximation. Hosea is a very peculiar prophet, because the message God entrusts to him does not pass only through words, but consists in a personal relationship: He is asked, in fact, to marry a prostitute, that is, to enter into an asymmetrical relationship, not based on mutual dignity, and to remain faithful to that relationship despite the obvious betrayal of the bride, given her professional activity. In chapter 2, in dialogue with the sons, who are brothers, God says:

Accuse your mother, accuse her,
for she is no longer my wife
and I am no longer her husband!
Remove from her face the marks of her prostitution
and the marks of her adultery from her breast;

or else I will strip her naked
And make her as she was when she was born
And I will reduce her to a wilderness, as a barren land,
and I will make her die of thirst.

Her children I will not love,
for they are the children of prostitution.

Their mother has prostituted herself,
Their parent has covered herself with shame.
She said, "I will follow my lovers,
who give me my bread and my water,
my wool, my flax,
my oil and my drink.⁶

The relational analysis immediately captures the intertwining of the spousal and filial relationship: If she has prostituted herself, the children are not the groom's, so that the children themselves are called in as witnesses. But in the words of the oracle the deepest dimension of that sign which is the desert also emerges: Here one is alone, without relationships, because in this "place" it is not possible to live. The reading of the Jewish people leads every effect

6   Hosea 2:4–7.

back to God, even the reduction of the bride, that is the mother, to a desert without water and therefore, paradoxically for a mother, deprived of life. This is the denial of identity caused by the denial of relationship. Tradition has learned to read these expressions in an etiological key, that is, as a revelation of the cause of the human being's death. In fact, God himself, while threatening, speaks of life, of rebirth. To be reduced as when one is born means to be stripped, but also to be disposed to regeneration. The problem is that the bride has sought life from idols, which cannot give life, because they are dead. A psalm states this clearly, in merciless words:

The idols of the people are silver and gold,
the work of human hands.
They have mouths and do not speak,
they have eyes and do not see,
they have ears and do not hear,
they have nostrils and do not smell.
They have hands and do not palpate,
they have feet and do not walk;
their throats make no sound.
Let him who makes them be like them
and whoever trusts in them.[7]

The desert is, therefore, the "place" of limit, where man touches the boundaries of his own existence. In this consists its ambivalence, which makes it an occasion of death, but also of life. Here Jesus is tempted by the devil precisely in His being the Son of God.[8] The challenge is totalizing, because it touches His body, His psyche and His spirit. To the former corresponds the temptation to turn stones

7   Psalm 114:4–8.
8   Cfr. Mat 4:1–11.

into bread, instead of letting His Father feed Him and, therefore, instead of remaining faithful to His Word, which constitutes the very identity of Christ. The invitation to throw oneself from the highest pinnacle of the temple, on the other hand, refers to the need for security in love, a temptation that Jesus expels once again with the Word of God which forbids tempting the One from whom one has radically received one's own origin as a gift. Finally, the offer of power over the whole earth in exchange for the adoration of the devil, who is a simple creature, touches the deepest, spiritual heart of the question, which basically revolves around the difference between God and idols. This is the most fundamental question, on which everything else depends. In fact, the awareness of the human being's identity also relates to it. If we are children of God in Christ the Son and His beloved creatures, then the answer to the question about His identity will contain the one about our identity and, therefore, about how to really live. But this implies that our body, our psyche and our spirit, that is, all of us, can never escape the risk of love, which is always a journey, a pilgrimage. The certainty of sustenance, the psychological security of being loved, and operational control over the world are the roots of that idolatrous tendency that leads to death, that is, in the opposite direction to that love to which we tend because we come from it.

Thus the desert can be the place where one learns to know God, distinguishing Him from idols like the golden calf, and, therefore, can be the place where one discovers oneself. This is why the very harsh words of Hosea's oracle include a strong hope:

Therefore, behold, I will bar your way with thorns
And I will encircle its enclosure with barriers.
And she will not find her paths again.

She will pursue her lovers,
but will not reach them,

She will search for them without finding them.
Then she will say, "I will return to my former husband
For I was happier than I am now".[9]

This judgment of the bride, who recognizes the "place" of happiness in her husband's home[10] through an operation of relational reflexivity, is precisely the deepest layer of the identity of the son, the daughter and the rational creature in general. In the parable of the prodigal son,[11] everything revolves around this judgment of the younger son, who asked his father to divide the money between him and his brother, in order to leave for a distant country, religiously inhabited by idols, as revealed by the fact that there he will end up grazing pigs, impure animals for the Jews. In that place he will find himself in an infra-human situation, because he will not even receive carobs, the food of the animals entrusted to him. His existence becomes merely functional: He is for the pigs and not the pigs for him. From a relational point of view, this kind of "desert" comes from the symbolic killing of the father. In fact, claiming the inheritance is equivalent to asking the father that he die prematurely. But after having squandered all his wealth, even with prostitutes, as his elder brother is careful to point out, the little brother discovers his true inheritance through the judgment that he shares with the prostitute wife of Hosea: "Then he came to his senses and said, 'How many wage earners in my father's house have bread in abundance, and I am starving here!'"[12] And returning thanks to this judgment of profit, which is the true inheritance because it is an act of relational reflexivity, he discovers that his father had never ceased to wait for him

9   Hosea 2:8–9.
10 It is *home* and not just *house* because it points to the relational, i.e. personal, dimension.
11 Cf. Lk 15:11–32.
12 Lk 15:17.

and to scan the horizon in search of him, like God who after the original sin cried out, "Adam, where are you?".[13] Returning, the son experiences who his father really is, this father who comes out to meet him and throws his arms around his neck, covering him once again with the signs of his identity. Thus the prodigal son discovers that his true substance was not the inheritance, but the unfailing relationship with his father.

This is the meaning of the desert, this is the reason for the forty years of the people and the forty days of Jesus. He is God who goes in "quarantine" in the place of the human being, to reveal the human being *to* the human being.[14] Thus Hosea's oracle itself is a hymn to identity and relationship:

Therefore, behold, I will draw her to me,
I will lead her into the desert
and I will speak to her heart.

I will make her vineyards
and I will turn the valley of Achor
into a gate of hope.
There she will sing
As in the days of her youth
as when she came out of the land of Egypt.

And it shall come to pass in that day
– oracle of the Lord – you shall call me: My husband,
And you shall no longer call me: My master.

I will take from your mouth
the names of the Baals

13   Gen 3:9.
14   Cf. Second Vatican Council, *Gaudium et Spes*, 22.

They shall no longer be remembered.
At that time I will make a covenant for them
with the beasts of the earth
and the birds of the sky
and with the reptiles of the ground;
bow and sword and war
I will remove from the land;
And I will make them rest easy.

I will make you my bride forever,
I will make you my wife
in righteousness and justice,
in kindness and in love,

I will betroth you to me in faithfulness
And you shall know the Lord.

On that day I will respond,
– oracle of the Lord
I will respond to the heavens,
and they shall respond to the earth;
The earth shall respond to the grain,
and wine, and oil,
and these shall respond to Jezreel.

I will sow them again for me in the land
and I will love Not-my-loved-one;
and to Not-my-people I will say, My people,
and they shall say unto me, My God.[15]

The poetic text shows how the desert is the "place" of the en-

15 Hosea 2:14–23.

counter with God, who wants to bring His creature there to speak to her heart, to transfigure the relationship with her, freeing her from every bondage. In the desert, one can discover that one is not alone, thanks to being alone with God, precisely because one has no shelter, nor is it possible to anesthetize or distract oneself. The desert is the point of crisis of the human heart, but in the literal sense of the Greek root of the term which means judgment (*krisis*). Freedom is not independence from judgment, as modernity has claimed, giving rise to a society in which everyone feels inadequate because they do not meet the expectations of an idolatrous culture, which causes death because its ideals are idols. Judgment is inescapable since it is constituted by the relationship with reality, with one's own identity and the identity of others. To be oneself means to be in a difference with others and, therefore, to be in a judgment. Thus, freedom does not consist in the absence of judgment, but depends radically on who judges, who founds the difference that constitutes our identity. The journey in the desert makes us move from *not* to *my*, from the rejection of the vital relationship with our Creator to the rebirth from the marvelous judgment that this word brings with it: *my* son, *my* father, *my* brother, *my* sister, *my* wife and husband, and so on for every true and vital relationship, which is summed up in the expression of abysmal depth, to which Jesus refers, "my neighbor."

Note that the text of Hosea also includes the earth in the rebirth of love, one might say in the resurrection of the relationship between the bridegroom and the bride. It is as if the earth is also drawn into the renewed dialogue between them. The animals of the soil and the sky, the grain, the wine and the oil enter into a choral song. In the face of the health crisis caused by the virus, this statement about the human being's relationship with the world becomes crucial, where again the etymology of the adjective (from *crux*, i.e. cross) is extremely significant. Life is radically a relationship that embraces the dimension of the person and that of the cosmos. And it is precisely the desert, and therefore also the evidence of the pandemic, that is the extreme "place" where one can experience such relationality, as Antoine de Saint-Exupéry wrote, in the light of his own history and with an allusion to Christ's encounter with the Samaritan woman:[16] "What makes the desert beautiful is the fact that it hides a well somewhere..."[17]

16 Cf. John 4:5–26.
17 A. Saint-Exupéry, *The Little Prince*, c. XXIV. The author specifies, in fact, that the well that the aviator and the Little Prince find in the desert is not like the wells of the Sahara, but looks like the well of a village.

3. The Unconscious Dialectical Matrix

A first, obvious objection that may arise when reading this little volume is: This is not science, here faith is needed! And this objection is well-founded. Theology is a form of thought that moves from an encounter, from the *yes* to the Word of God that reveals Himself. In the data from which one thinks, the personal relationship with God enters in, which, precisely because it is personal, is not *a priori*. We are not proceeding from abstract axioms, but we are working *a posteriori* from the observation of what happened during and after the pandemic at the anthropological level, theologically reflecting on it through the scientific and phenomenological analysis proposed by Pierpaolo Donati. He indicated the relationship as a fundamental element through which the pandemic has brought about an epiphany. This last term has Christmas resonances, recalling the Three Kings, wise men, scientists we would call them today, who by observing the sky found Christ. At the entrance of the Cathedral of Como, in Italy, a magnificent work of art dating back to 1396, the main portal is flanked by two sculptures that to the untrained eye may appear as two saints, but in reality, they are two pagans: Pliny the Elder, a naturalist, and Pliny the Younger, his nephew, a humanist, both originally from Como. In the lunette of the same entrance portal is represented a magnificent adoration of the Magi, evidence of strong devotion linked to the stopover in the city of Barbarossa who transported their relics. All these iconographic choices suggest that natural sciences and humanities can both be paths that lead to the encounter with Christ.

The reference to the facade of the Cathedral of Como, my city of origin, is not only the result of parochialism or sentimental memory of my father's explanations when I was a child, but a concrete illustration of the result of a different cultural matrix than the one we have today. Just think what we would think if a new church were built with statues of two non-believing scientists on the facade. The same objection that may arise spontaneously as we move on with the present analysis is the consequence of a worldview that tends not only to distinguish, as is right, but also, unfortunately, to separate the scientific and the theological and spiritual spheres. In doing so, one does not prescind from religious discourse, one simply does not see it anymore, because one no longer recognizes the action of idols that, in some cases, also take on the guise of scientific theories. As a matter of fact, a common experience during this period of health crisis was the impossibility to understand the discordant statements of the different scientists appearing on television. The perplexity of the listener in search of safe guidelines stemmed from not being able to find the exactitude that should distinguish scientific work from opinions based on faith or religious belief or superstition. "It's a simple flu", but "No, it's like the bubonic plague", and "Everyone has to wear a mask", or rather "No, only the sick", and again, "It's necessary to go into lock-down", but "It was a mistake" and so on. The point in calling this "up the mask, down the mask" is not to defame science. The author, as noted above, has a doctorate in theoretical physics as well as a doctorate in theology. Instead, we want to highlight how even medicine finds its "desert", i.e. touches its limit. Thus, the claim of salvation exclusively through science is one of the idols fallen in front of the babble and brawls of its "oracles" on the various talk shows.

On the contrary, the strength of Donati's scientific approach is his ability to recognize relational causality in social phenomena, thus going back to the ontological density of the relationship itself, in order to critically examine the cultural matrix underlying the observed reality. Without such relational reflexivity one runs the risk of not even being aware of the cultural matrix in which one moves. When I was working as a physicist, one of my colleagues, a Russian Jew, told me that in Siberia, when something went wrong, they said that it was the fault of the Jews or the cyclists, to which I asked, "Why the cyclists?" and I was answered, "Why the Jews?". Although I abhor anti-Semitism, which I think is profoundly stupid, I take it for granted that there are those who think this way, because somehow it is present in the cultural matrix of the Western society in which we are immersed, which fears differences and tries to erase them. For the analysis proposed in this small volume, it may be interesting to note, by the way, that anti-Semitism historically developed most strongly when church and state were closest. Indeed, clericisation made it difficult to distinguish the citizen from the Christian.

But this undermines the very foundation of the relationship, which unites and distinguishes at the same time and for the same reason, as happens, for example, in the relationship between a father and a son, or between a professor and his students. Donati's relational approach, on the other hand, makes possible the dialogue of sociology with a science such as theology, which thinks within a web of relationships that claim to have their origin in the personal relationship with the First Principle itself. The God of Jesus Christ, His *Abba*, is the God of Abraham, Isaac and Jacob, the God of the fathers. But besides that, the relational approach is also a basis for dialogue with philosophy and between the various sciences, which are increasingly autistically closed in hyper-specialization, the results of which are there for all to see.[18] The clinician,

18 On this approach, see: P. Donati – A. Malo – G. Maspero (Eds.), *Social Science, Philosophy and Theology in Dialogue: A Relational Perspective*, (Routledge, London 2019).

the virologist and the epidemiologist have often failed to understand each other, while the fate of the world was entrusted to them. This even led to talk of an infodemic, because the excess of information and its contradictory nature was taking on a toxicity comparable to that of the pandemic itself.

But on the theological side, it is possible to lean on an element that has already emerged, highlighted by the journey of the Magi themselves, which in a natural way constitutes a platform for dialogue with the other critical approaches to reality: creation. We have seen how the oracle of Hosea joins the marriage covenant and the cosmic covenant between the human being and nature. This is so from the very first pages of Genesis, which obviously cannot be read as if it were a scientific treatise, but which at the same time conveys what of the scientific enterprise is the basis: the possibility of relating to the causes of what is known. For this reason, the correct reading of this text is etiological, i.e. it refers to the search for the causes of reality: Essentially, we are told that the world is not God, but that it has a sense, it has a regular structure, whose laws we can search for, because it originated from a God who imprinted such a logic, such a *logos*, in it.

When we speak of musicology, technology, sociology and so on, we refer to a scientific discourse (*logos*) that has as its object the reality indicated by the first part of the expression. But this research is made possible by a real structure inherent in the reality itself studied. The cultural matrix of a society explains precisely this structure, and therefore constitutes the frame of reference within which the world acquires meaning. Even if this frame of reference is historically expressed in religious terms, it can be observed independently of the acceptance or rejection of them. This is what happens when one takes a comparative perspective. Thus, it is possible to juxtapose the origin-of-the-world narrative of Babylon, that of ancient Greece, and that of the Bible, regardless of whether one accepts these traditions as true.

In the *Enūma Eliš*, a poem in Akkadian probably dating back to the twelfth century BC, everything begins with an original couple, Apsû, the abyss, and his bride, Tiāmat, goddess of the salt waters and mother of the cosmos and all the gods. The sons, however, disturb their progenitors, moving their father to the decision to kill them. But one of his descendants, Ea, manages to kill Apsû, after putting him to sleep and depriving him of the crown. From Ea and his goddess wife Damkina was born the god Marduk, who leads a host of gods against Tiāmat, wife of the deceased Apsû, placed at the head of another army also composed of gods. In the terrible clash, the universal mother tries to swallow Ea, which, however, manages to tear the bowels of the goddess and pierce her heart. Then, dissecting the corpse, Ea creates the world with its different parts. For example, from the saliva originate the clouds, from the skull are made to flow the Tigris and the Euphrates, from the chest are drawn mountains and so on. But to create the human beings Marduk must kill a bad god, allied by the now defeated Tiāmat, so that from the spilled blood takes origin the humanity.[19]

The first thing that jumps to the eye following the narrative is that it seems like a mafia war. At the beginning of everything there is a cosmic couple, personification of the duality that characterizes the world. The conflict arises from the multiplicity that through this couple comes to being, until a final clash, which after a patricide leads to the killing of the mother of the gods, ready to swallow his challenger. Nature would derive from her body and the human beings from the blood of those who were allied with her. The dialectic is evident.

If we turn to the Greek world, according to the reconstruction of the *Bibliotheca*, a mythographic collection erroneously attributed to Apollodorus of Athens, from the second century BC, but

19 Cf. W.G. Lambert, *Babylonian Creation Myths* (Ann Arbor, MI: Eisenbrauns, 2013).

in truth dating from the second century AD, the cultural matrix underlying the narrative does not seem to differ much from the previous one. The first lord of the world is Uranus, who marries Gaea, by whom he has numerous children. Among them are the Cyclops, with one eye in the middle of the forehead. The father, however, fears them so much as to put them in chains and lock them in the Tartarus. Then Uranus has from Gaea other sons, the Titans, the youngest of which is Kronos. The mother, angry at the loss of the Cyclops, persuades the Titans to attack Uranus and gives the youngest a scythe of steel, with which he emasculates Uranus, dethroning him and freeing his brothers. But history repeats itself, because even Kronos is afraid of the Cyclops and locks them again in the Tartarus. So he marries his sister Rhea, but swallows all the children he has with her, because his mother and father had prophesied that a son would take away his power. So Kronos swallows Pluto and Poseidon. Rhea, of course, is angry about this, so when she is pregnant with Zeus, she flees to Crete and gives birth to him in a cave, then entrusting him to the nymphs. She gives Kronos a stone wrapped in swaddling clothes for him to swallow, thinking that it is his newborn son. The war goes on for ten years, until Gaea predicts that Zeus will have the victory only by allying himself with the Cyclops, who give him the lightning, as well as a helmet to Pluto and the trident to Poseidon. With these weapons Zeus defeats his father and shares the power with the allies, taking control of the sky, while Pluto takes the governance of Hades and Poseidon that of the sea.[20]

It is evident that the relational structure is very similar to the Babylonian narrative, because the dialectic in the transition from the original couple to the descendants is unchanged. Paternity, spousality and filiation appear irreconcilable. Here it is the father

20 Cf. R. Hard, *Apollodorus: The Library of Greek Mythology* (Oxford: Oxford University Press, 1997).

who swallows the children and the reproduction of the clash from generation to generation is more evident. But the world always originates from a couple and from a couple's crisis, with the dialectic that follows from generation. The divinities are personifications of the natural powers, of which they maintain the conflictual dimension.

The mythological clash between father and son is refined and exemplified in the tragedies, among which the *Oedipus Rex* cycle is paradigmatic. In Sophocles' narration, the enlightened sovereign discovers in a single day that the epidemic afflicting his city is caused by the fact that he himself killed his father Laius and married his mother Jocasta. Significantly, the son killed his father at a crossroads on the road between Thebes and Delphi. The relational collapse due to the disappearance of the differences between father and son, mother and bride, makes the city unlivable, cutting at the root the possibility of sociality.

And this tragic effect is transmitted to Oedipus' children, as narrated in *Antigone*, where his daughter finds herself trapped in the tragic knot between the law of the city *(polis)* and that of the family *(genos)*. If we want to avoid anachronistic readings of the work of Sophocles, we are not faced with a romantic heroine, but with the impossibility of obeying two laws that are as absolute as they are irreconcilable. In fact, seven valiant champions had attacked Thebes, where Creon, Oedipus' brother, had become tyrant, and had been confronted by seven other champions, who defended the city. In the clash one of Antigone's brothers had found himself facing another brother and, as must happen in a tragedy, the two had killed each other. Euripides narrated it in his *The Seven Against Thebes*, around 467 BC. Twenty-five years later Sophocles makes us participants in the dilemma of the sister, who as a citizen is subjected to the decision of Creon that the corpses of the fallen attackers be left to the birds of the air, a decision that had ominous consequences for the fate in the afterlife of the deceased. But she, as a sister, must bury both her fallen brother defending Thebes and the one who had attacked it. This relational "cross" also includes Aemon, son of Creon and Antigone's fiancé, who intercedes for her with his father, invoking natural law and reason that protects the innocent. But the ruler's argument is that if his son and his family members, i.e. the *genos*, did not obey the law of the *polis*, then the city itself would cease to exist, because no one would obey anymore, not even in battle. This is the same conflict that leads the seemingly perfect Athenian *polis* to decree the death of Socrates.

The Greek example is extremely significant and it is no coincidence that it can be considered the foundation of Western thought. We still have a narrative structure that emphasizes dialectics, but now the metaphysical (a) and social (b) foundations of the mythology are more explicit.

The conflict between the father and the sons, with the ensuing duel, can be traced back to the tension between the one and the many, which from Parmenides and Heraclitus marks Greek philosophical reflection. Metaphysics itself arises from what Plato described in the Sophist as the "patricide" of Parmenides. Being cannot be considered only in a univocal sense, as the latter claimed, because the many do exist and are not pure appearance. Then it is necessary to reread the myth, bringing out the rational content behind the veil of narratives, to show that being is considered analogically. This has a fundamental impact on the very possibility of knowledge, which according to Parmenides was scientific (*episteme*), i.e. true, only if it prescinded from the multiple, a field for him marked in an ineluctable way by pure opinability (*doxa*). In the Platonic reading, on the other hand, analogy allowed scientific knowledge even in the dimension characterized by multiplicity, through the dialectical analysis.

The metaphysical reading of mythological patricide also allows us to glimpse the social value of the issue, which is revealed precisely in the relational tensions. The family appears at the heart of the most ancient narratives, which try to give reasons for the foundation of human sociality, without success. But the greatness of Greek humanism consists precisely in giving the honor of art to the victims of tragedy, covering with eternal beauty the fallen in the conflict between the different laws, for the impossibility of connecting the one and the many. There are no words to pay homage to a thought that recognizes its own limits and hands them down in an imperishable form as pity for the victims. The Greek soul is, therefore, pierced by this tension, which shows how culturally deep the theological analysis of the sociological data could be when it approaches the family and human relationships.

4. The Revealed Relational Matrix

But what is to be found in the Judaeo-Christian framework? Here, proceeding in a comparative way, regardless of aprioristic positions, one discovers that the text proposes a narrative that is decidedly different and irreducible to the previous ones. The first chapter of Genesis, commonly believed to date from the sixth century BC, already presents a radical novelty in its *incipit*, because from an original couple we pass to an evident monism. The statement "In the beginning God created the heavens and the earth"[21] has in fact three elements: (a) God in the beginning (*bārē'šît 'ĕlōhîm*); (b) the act of creating (*bārā'*); (c) the pair of heaven and earth (*'ēt haššā-mayim wa'ēt hā'āres*). So we have an absolute principle that is unique and is identified with God, we might say on high. And this unique principle places an act vertically, expressed with a verb that can only have Him as its subject, precisely because it is radically vertical. From this act originate the heavens and the earth, and a couple is the object of this action, in the lower horizontal dimension. What was vertical in the Babylonian and Greek conception is now only horizontal, because an absolutely transcendent dimension has been opened up.

This first verse would be enough to illustrate the extraordinary metaphysical novelty that a small people, essentially shepherds, managed to introduce before Parmenides and Plato. The question as to the reason for such an extraordinary leap would require a theological discourse in its own right; suffice it to say that the narrative

---

21 Gen 1:1.

itself attributes all that it knows of God to an encounter the fathers had with Him. Here, comparatively, and therefore relationally, we limit ourselves to observing that the "two" is no longer original, but everything draws its origin from a unique Subject who freely poses an act that only He can pose. The novelty of this element is confirmed by the observation that dialectics is entirely absent from the Jewish explanation of how the cosmos originated.

The continuation of the narrative makes this clear, because the first five verses, in which the first day of creation is explained, indicate the latter not with the cardinal adjective, but with the numeral one: It is the day "one" (*ehād*), not the "first." This is fundamental because the cardinal adjective can only be said if there is a two, i.e. a second. Instead, the beginning of which we speak is absolute and from this radical unity all the rest, the multiple, is presented as a gift and fruit of the immanent life of God who performs five actions: (1) creates, (2) says, (3) sees, (4) distinguishes, and (5) calls. God first of all brings about creation, an action expressed through the verb *bara'* (1), but this happens through His word, because it is enough for Him to say (the verb is *amar*) "let there be light!" for there to be light (2).[22] This creation through speaking refers back to God's interiority, connecting the visible and external world to a *logos*, a thought, which the Christian tradition will later reread as the Word who, according to the Father's plan, becomes flesh as the first and last meaning of creation.[23] Here already emerges the Trinitarian foundation of creation itself which, thanks to Gospel revelation, it is possible to grasp *a posteriori*. The subsequent actions of this unique Principle belong to the same track, or subtrack,[24]

---

22 Gen 1:3.
23 See, for example, the magnificent text by Maximus the Confessor, *Quaestiones ad Thalassium*, q. 22.
24 In the light of what has been said about the difference between numerals and ordinals, it would be theologically incorrect to call God

because they express a judgment (3) on the result of the creative act, which is seen (the verb is *raah*) to be "good" (*towb*) and, therefore, is distinguished (the verb here is *badal*, the Greek *diechôrisen* of the Septuagint) by the Creator Himself into two realities (4) which are light and darkness, called by Him (the verb is *qara*) day and night (5).

From the Trinitarian point of view, therefore, reading the Bible "from the end" as a single text, it is important to note that God speaks the first words only after the reader has become acquainted with the Spirit, who hovers over the waters. Reality, in fact, can only respond to the Creator if it is placed under the Spirit of God. This relationship is a gift from above. The world thus arose as a liturgy and is a liturgy because day and night continue to respond to God who calls them, in such a way that time itself, seen here in its origin, can be read as a response to God. Life, human history, the tides, the clouds passing through the sky, everything is dialogue.

From the same perspective one can highlight the importance of the divine judgment that declares good what God has created and immediately, as indicated by the simple copula that connects the two actions, is translated by the Creator into a further action. This consists in the distinction that brings out a pair that is no

the 'first principle', as the Aristotelian tradition has taught us to do, because the unmoved mover is first insofar as it is the first element of a chain that necessarily includes a second and then a third, and so on down the scale of moved movers, increasingly imperfect as one moves away from the first. The Creator, on the other hand, is not bound to the world. This question is fundamental to Trinitarian theology, because when we refer to the first divine Person we are saying something radically different from Aristotle, in that the Son is coeternal with the Father and the Spirit, and is not merely the second step in an ontological hierarchy that necessarily unites God and the cosmos.

longer merely original, but now originating, i.e. the source of other couples. In fact, in the following days the pattern repeats itself, as multiplicity appears as the result of the creative act, that is as the fecundity of divine unity. On the second day, in fact, the five verbs are repeated, because God speaks to create the firmament which He calls heaven and then distinguishes between the waters above and those below. Then on the third day in the waters below the heavens the pair of the earth and the sea is constituted and judged good as a relationship. From the earth the Creator causes vegetation to arise, introducing a further distinction, which again leads to the judgment of goodness. This is repeated for the next pairs, the day and the night, with their respective sun and moon regulating them. From the comparative point of view, it is apparent that for the Jewish people of the sixth century BC, the natural realities that refer to the main deities in the pagan sphere are recognized as mere creatures. On the sixth day, after the creation of the animals of the sky and of the seas, each according to its own species, therefore still in relation, if we do not let ourselves be misled in the reading by evolutionary concerns, we reach the climax with the creation of yet another couple, introduced by a solemn formula in which God speaks in the plural, because it is a creation in His own image and likeness, so much so that this must be the head of all other creatures: "God created man in his own image; in the image of God he created him; male (*zakar*) and female (*neqebah*) he created them."[25] The verb *bara'* is solemnly repeated three times because we are in the deepest core of meaning of the creation narrative: the one Principle of all things expresses Himself by placing out of Himself creatures that He Himself judges to be good, because they are relational, to the extreme of infusing His own image and likeness into that dust of which the next chapter speaks in the narrative that, however, chronologically most likely origi-

25   Gen 1:27.

nated three centuries earlier. The point is crucial because this last step marks a qualitative change in the whole of creation which is no longer just good, but is now judged by God to be very good (*meod towb*).[26] Here we clearly see in action a cultural and theological matrix profoundly different from the Babylonian and Greek cosmogonies. Yet mythological and tragic elements remain in the text, such as the references to the garden and the serpent, or the divine punishment of Pharaoh who, like a new Oedipus, took as his wife the beautiful Sarai, whom Abram out of fear said was his sister when he went down to Egypt to escape a famine.[27] Again, the issue is at the same time metaphysical and social: human relationality is presented as an expression of God's uniqueness and as the meaning of all creation, structured precisely in couples that are founded in the One who is God. Here there is no conflict between the one and the many because, in a certain way, in the light of evangelical revelation, we can recognize the relationship already in God, as John will do later by focusing the beginning of his gospel on the creation in six days and, in particular, by recalling in the *incipit* of his narration the *incipit* of Genesis. One could say that the creation narrative really closes with the first verses of John: "In the beginning was the Word, and the Word was with God, and the Word was God. He was in the beginning with God: all things were made through Him, and without Him nothing was made of all that exists."[28] Nothing was created without the *Logos*, which is not only the Word of God, but which is God, because Son, that is, Relation which reveals God Himself as Father, who in turn is Relation.

One could say that creation itself bears within itself a cross, because the multiplicity that characterizes it is an expression of the

26 Gen 1:31.
27 Cf. Gen 12:10–20.
28 John 1:1–3.

infinite origin that is the unity and uniqueness of its Creator.[29] Thus the horizontal relationality in the world can never find its own fulfillment, if not by ascending vertically towards its own source which is the one and triune God. The enigma of the relationship is a consequence of the mystery in the proper and theological sense that man carries within himself, insofar as he who is finite was created in the image of the infinite God, so much so that he cannot help but always tend towards that beyond. But this constant referral is founded in the very metaphysics of the human being and the world.

The continuation of the Genesis narrative shows this in two passages. First, in the second chapter, it illustrates how man, despite having all of creation at his disposal, is alone. God, after having created the garden of Eden, with four rivers including the Tigris and the Euphrates, fills it with all sorts of animals and presents them to man so that he can give them a name. But the world, for him, is still a desert. Thus, the Creator, after having said that "It is not good that man should be alone,"[30] brings down a torpor on Adam from whose breast he molds Eve. The man, contemplating the woman, in paying her the first compliments in history, which in this case can also be read in a Eucharistic perspective, in the sense that they are thanksgiving to God, recognizes the relationship that unites them.

In the light of all this, the initial verse of Genesis, which presents the one God who gives origin to heaven and earth, that is, who imprints relationality on creation as an expression of His own unity, finds in the final redaction of the biblical text its fulfillment in that "and the two shall be one flesh,"[31] which allows them to be

29 Perhaps this 'cross' was what Jesus was referring to in the words in Lk 14:25–27.
30 Gen 2:18.
31 Gen 2:24.

themselves, that is, to stand in their own naked identity without shame. Man and woman are called to leave their parents not dialectically, but to constitute a relational unity, which is made possible in the unity and oneness of God. In the third chapter it is this relational fulfillment that is attacked by the serpent, so much so that, after sin, the man and woman are ashamed of their nakedness and dialectic enters their relationship.[32] One could say that creation becomes again for the human being to a certain extent a desert.[33] But, as we have said, God continues to seek man and that "Adam, where are you?" will be translated into the *Logos* becoming flesh in order to re-establish the relationship with the Father, with woman and with the brothers.

This exegetical path aims to show how the Judeo-Christian cultural matrix recognizes relationship in the very depths of the world, as a trace of the relational source that is the Creator. The tension between one's own finiteness and the infinite desire which runs through the heart of every human being, is not a condemnation, but on the contrary a sign of outstanding dignity, because it is a consequence of creation in the image and likeness of the triune God. Whenever this infinite desire is folded into a finite object, there is idolatry and a gash of desert is reopened in the world. In fact, the sociality of the human being has a precise metaphysical root which cannot be evaded, unless at the price of losing oneself. It seems significant that the tragedy of Oedipus takes place precisely during an epidemic, similar to the age we are living in. The theological proposal put forward here, starting from sociological

32 Cf. Gen 3:11–12.
33 Something similar happens with the universal flood, narrated in Gen 6, when that relational space between the waters above and the waters below, opened by the act of creation, will close. Only Noah's ark, that is, the space preserved by the vertical relationship with the transcendent God, will allow the different pairs of living beings to survive.

analysis, is that such a "desert" can help us to have the socio-metaphysical experience that limits and differences are not a problem when we are in relationship, because the limits themselves can be recognized as thresholds, through which viruses can pass, but thresholds that for the same reason have the power to make us discover the depth of human relationality. And this leads to a true source of being, and therefore of life, from which creation itself is structured and founded.

5. The Original Tension and Idolatry

The original narrative that characterizes the Judeo-Christian matrix presents creation, even in its material and bodily dimension, as radically constituted by both immanent and transcendent relationships, posed and ordered by God's own action. This is important from a secular point of view: the claim is to give an account of the deepest sense of reality as every human being can see it, and not as only a chosen few might do, after having been introduced into an esoteric sphere. This is a "secular" principle, in the deepest sense, because here we are talking about the very creation of the *saecula*, that is, of centuries and time, which are presented as a response to the Creator's word. This makes it possible to dialogue with non-believers as well, starting from the common object of knowledge that is reality, independently of the positions of faith of each one. In this sense, the Judaeo-Christian matrix invokes the comparison with concrete existence as its own criterion of truth, without claiming to be true *a priori*. The foundation of this characteristic is precisely its relationality, which does not enclose the phenomenon within itself, but launches it towards the other, founding identity simultaneously in the vertical relationship with the transcendent Creator and horizontally with the immanent multiplicity of others.

This justifies the very idea of this volume, which tests the relational interpretive hypothesis about the social phenomenon that emerged in the pandemic crisis. But then the question at stake here is: Does what manifests itself to observation seem to be more in accord with the Babylonian matrix, the Greek matrix, or the biblical matrix? I think that one would be tempted to say that families today may be reminiscent of the very conflictuality of the first two examples cited. The same lock-down has detonated more than one "Babylon" in the family web around us. But is that all there is to it? Hasn't more emerged? Let me give you an immediate example: Haven't we discovered that we cannot live alone and that we need physical contact, even just a handshake? Hasn't deprivation also shown us a positive reality, an irrepressible dimension of our desire?

Herein lies the central point of the present interpretative proposal. If what is narrated in Genesis is true, in the etiological sense illustrated, then the same dialectic, which is found at every turn in our concrete lives, can find a relational explanation. But to get to this point, it is necessary to introduce the notion of idol and illustrate its origin, according to the same Judeo-Christian matrix to which we are referring.

We have seen how the principle of everything is not a horizontal pair with the consequent conflict with respect to the multiplicity that is generated by it, but everything is created by the one God through a vertical transcendent relationship whose power and reality is expressed generatively in the multiplicity that originates from it, through a structure of horizontal pairs, rooted "above". In other words, the conflict between the original couple and the resulting multiplicity is defused by the unity in which the same couple is founded.[34]

As mentioned, this structure, mediated by the creation "in the image and likeness" of God, expressions of the content, precisely, relational, constitutes the human being, who as a creature is finite, but among creatures is distinguished because she is constitutively

---

34 Jesus' own double commandment to love first God above all things and then one's neighbour as oneself (cf. Mat 22:37–40 and parallels) expresses this relational order.

placed in relation with the infinite. This is like an original, profound and inescapable cross that marks the heart of each one. Here originates the possibility of dialectic without limits, which characterizes the human animal, unlike other animals, for which the instinct necessarily marks an insurmountable boundary to the conflict. From this point of view, the double component of the relationship of *religo* (to bind) and *refero* (to refer), highlighted by Donati, can be presented as a refraction of the finite immanent dimension (*religo*), which precisely binds the couple in relation, and the infinite transcendent dimension (*refero*), which always sends man beyond himself. The "desert" from which we began finds here its most radical foundation: The human being is ontologically in tension between an origin and a beyond, and for this reason he must always leave his own land, his own home, to find his own land and his own home not in a place, but in the relationship with his Creator which founds him in the most intimate way. For this reason the finite, any finite, is not enough for him. Man's life has an "exodic" structure, in the sense that he must always set out as a pilgrim. In biblical terms, every man is a "Jew", i.e. *ivrit*, a technical term that designates the member of the chosen people and means "one who crosses". The expression "wandering Jew", after all, is a tautology, but it expresses the truest identity of every human being, who is himself only in the continuous search for a beyond. In the technical terminology introduced, he is, therefore, he belongs (*religo*), only in referring to a reality that transcends him (*refero*). This means that the place I belong to is always beyond. Creation, after all, shows us the relational identity of each of us, that is the sense of the world itself, for our creation in God's image and likeness. In Christ, then, these two terms can be reread as a reference to filiation in the Son, who is the heart of the world.

All this is immediately connected to the possibility of idolatry, because the insufficiency of every creaturely reality, for its intrinsic finitude, leads man to symbolically project the beyond onto a reality that falls within his own sphere of action and is therefore controllable. Being the image of God implies the impossibility of being secure and satisfied in substances, because, as for the prodigal son, only a relationship can respond to the implacable cry of one's heart. This opens up the space for idolatrous temptation, which consists in a manipulative act whose aim is to feel secure and satisfied. Think of the chosen people in the desert during the exodus: They saw the Red Sea open up before them, the Egyptian horsemen succumb, food descend from the sky, and yet they did not resist during the absence of Moses, who was speaking with God face to face and then returning with the tables of the Law. They build themselves a golden calf to feel secure. They make themselves an image of God. Keep in mind that they were not thinking of another deity at that time, but the sin of idolatry is to produce an image of the one God with their own head and hands.[35] Instead, only God can be the image of God and this Image is the Son. Therefore only Jesus of Nazareth is the image of the true God, an image that is all of the Father and all of Mary, a woman, daughter of Eve. Significantly, He who is Relationship in eternity because He is Son of God, becomes son of man in the relationship of Mary with her Creator.

When we try to eliminate the tension towards the beyond by grasping onto a created substance, we end up in idolatry, which is not the simple violation of a law, the overcoming of a barrier. The triune God created us, in fact, to always go beyond. Unlike Hercules, the Christian can and must explore what lies beyond the namesake columns, as Christopher Columbus did with three ships, one of which was named *Santa Maria*. The drama of idolatry is the replacement of reality with an image. "Idol" comes, in fact, from the Greek verb *eidein*, which means to see. Reality has infinite depth precisely because of its immanent relational structure that

35 Cf. Ex 32.

refers back to the transcendent relational foundation. Instead, the idol is static and, above all, it is false, purely mental. It is a parasite of thought that takes the place of the relational source, giving an apparent peace because it does not have the depth of that source. The idol does not disturb, it reassures. But then it makes us slaves, dependent.

It is enough to read the third chapter of Genesis to see the device in action: From the very beginning in the dialogue with Eve, the serpent disfigures reality, subtly suggesting that God has forbidden eating of every tree in the garden. One immediately notices how his strategy is to distract from the relationship in order to draw attention to the substances. In response to Eve's correction, the deformation of the image, that is the rape of thought and the attack on relational virginity, comes into action. The woman leaves room within herself for the hypothesis that God is not as He is, but is according to an extrinsic image and not according to what she has experienced in her relationship with Him. Adam and Eve were created to be, in mutual relationship, the image and likeness of God. That is, they are already like Him. God cannot be afraid of this, because He gave it in the beginning. Indeed, the whole garden, that is, the world, every substance, belongs to them through this real relationship. Original sin has nothing to do with lust or mere disobedience to a command. Instead, it has to do with reality, because it is putting a mind-created idea above the reality created by God, starting from the idea of self. The progenitors, in making room for satanic substantive thinking, abdicate their relational thinking as children of God. The idea says that one can be oneself alone, reality shows that one can only be oneself in relationship, through the radical relationship with divine transcendence and then through the reciprocal relationship in the immanence of creation. In other words, the meaning of the command not to eat of the tree of life was not that God wanted to deprive them of the very life He had given them, but on the contrary it is simply the translation of the fact that constitutively, ontologically, life can only be received as a gift from another, in a relationship. In the final analysis, original sin is against filiation, which is why Jesus said that in order to enter the Kingdom of Heaven one must become like a child, for whom receiving is spontaneous and natural.[36]

To grasp the depth of what is described in the third chapter of Genesis, it is enough to compare it to the temptations of Christ in the desert, during his Lent, his "quarantine". As we have seen, they embrace the totality of His humanity, for the request to prove to Satan His filiation to the Father by turning stones into bread calls into question the body with its need to be nourished,[37] the challenge to throw Himself from the highest pinnacle of the temple refers to the psyche and its need for security,[38] while the offer of all the power in the world in exchange for adoration appeals to the spirit and to the fundamental religious question of who deserves adoration.[39] In all three of these temptations, the tragicomic dimension becomes evident as we consider that Jesus already has everything the devil offers Him. Everything is already His, just as Adam and Eve had already been given everything by the Creator, who evidently nourished them and loved them precisely because He had created them. Thus, in the Genesis narrative, when Eve turns her attention to the fruit of the tree of life, she realizes that it is "good to eat, pleasing to the eye and desirable for acquiring wisdom".[40] Here again we touch on the somatic dimension of food, the psychic dimension of aesthetic beauty and, finally, the spiritual dimension of wisdom. The Samaritan woman at the well in

36 Cf. Mat 18:1–10.
37 Cf. Mat 4:3.
38 Cf. Mat 4:5–6.
39 Cf. Mat 4:8–9.
40 Cf. Gen 3:6.

dialogue with Christ will make the same journey, starting from the somatic need for water, to open her heart to the psychic question of her love, to the more deeply spiritual question of where to worship.[41] But her thirst brings her back to that purity in her relationship with reality that Eve had lost. Thus the comparison with the "desert" of Christ is important because it highlights the inversion between reality and thought that takes place in the heart of the progenitors, wounding the deepest fibers of their being.

The essence of original sin is, therefore, the placing of thought above the relationship with reality, in an attempt to satisfy in a non-relational way, by oneself, that infinite desire inscribed in the human heart. From a philosophical point of view, this recalls the modern parable that moves from the operation of Descartes, who from a gnoseological perspective called the act of thinking as proof of one's existence, up to the idealist reinterpretation, which with Hegel translates the operation onto the ontological plane. Cartesian thinking is not in itself anti-relational, because it thinks something external to the subject, but when being is identified with the very thinking of the subject then the metaphysical matrix that arises can only be anti-relational. From here we deduce that idolatry, from a certain moment onwards, is intrinsic to the modern matrix, because what the subject thinks takes the place of what is, similarly to what happened to the thought of the progenitors at the moment they sinned.

The question is properly modern, because the difference with respect to ancient Greece is radical: There being was identified with the idea (Plato) or with the intelligible form (Aristotle), but as a universal and not as the thought of the subject, which had not yet been discovered before the encounter with Christianity.[42] On the

41 Cf. John 4:4–26.
42 Let us try the experiment of reading Augustine's *Confessions* in parallel with earlier and contemporary works.

other hand, in the Judeo-Christian matrix, the personal relationship with God and with His *Logos* who became flesh made it possible to recognize the human being as a subject endowed with an interiority. With modernity, the ontological closure in thinking traps the subject in himself, excluding him from the relational dimension. In other words, man, who has discovered himself to be a subject by speaking face to face with God, and therefore in a personal relationship with Him, believes that he can be self-founded, remaining enclosed in that mental dimension which is transformed into a pantheon of idols.

In the light of this, if one wishes, one can reinterpret the lockdowns caused by the pandemic as the realization in the concrete existence of the common human being of the modern individualist project that arose from the reworking of Descartes' operation. From here immediately follows the observation that in a paradoxical way this traumatic experience has provoked a rejection of this project and an awareness of the inhumanity of self-foundation.

Thus the pandemic can be presented as a catalyst for the crisis of modernity, already declared by the various post-modern projects present in contemporary culture. These arise from the rejection of those conflicts that modernity itself has exalted. On the other hand, the absolutization of the individual could not lead to anything else, as the example of the wars of the gods, that is, of the idols, suggests. When being is reduced to clear and distinct ideas, there is no more room for relational mediation that always transcends both identity and dialectics. Instead, reality is always richer, exceeding the human capacity to grasp it conceptually. In the moment in which being is identified with the thought of the human subject, all this richness is lost.

But the relationship, in its double structure of binding (*religo*) and referring (*refero*), simultaneously calls into question identity and difference, as well as immanence and transcendence. For this reason it is not reducible to a mere concept. Thus, that post-modern solution, which criticizes modernity not in its principles, but for the insufficient radicality in applying them, and aims to eliminate conflict by denying differences, is destined to generate even more conflicts, as the war that followed the pandemic showed. Given that differences exist in reality, relativizing them paradoxically abandons people to the dialectic itself, because it deprives them of the ability to think about them. Instead, it is urgent and necessary to learn how to relate differences, that is, to discover the dimension of the referent, the call to a "beyond" that is necessarily always "other", and for this reason can be a place of encounter and not only of clash. Otherwise, the progression from pandemic to war is a foregone conclusion.

The modern formula "my freedom ends where the other's begins" is radically insufficient, as this pandemic has shown experimentally. Closed in ourselves, in our homes, in our spaces, we should have all been as free as before. Instead, we have felt a great loss of freedom, invoking the possibility of meeting for a drink or giving each other a hug as constituent elements of a freedom that is not merely theoretical, but real. Perhaps in this lock-down we have experienced, through deprivation, that freedom is relationship. Modern freedom, insofar as it is mental and negative, can be compared precisely to the desert, in which one can go wherever one wants, but has nowhere to go and no one to meet. And yet, this same experience can help us rediscover the transcendence of relationships which, insofar as they are horizontal traces of the vertical source, present themselves as a real novelty of being. The leap is qualitative, because it is ontological. The relationship between two persons is not reducible to them, but introduces between them an ontological novelty that is real and habitable. Thus the land between people who enter into relationship is sacred, because it makes life possible.

Perhaps a playful example can serve to illustrate the metaphysical novelty. Just after the lock-down in Rome, close to the Vatican, a mural appeared with Tom and Jerry, both wearing masks, where the mouse invoked social distancing in front of the disconsolate cat. If modernity were *sic et simpliciter* right, the lock-down should have evaporated the dialectical dimension. But it didn't. What's more, we like Tom and Jerry because we know that, deep down, they are friends and, even if they fight, they do so because they are in a relationship. So a man and a woman who get married do not join some kind of fitness club or start a union negotiation, but enter together into a new territory, a new world, which their mutual *yes* in a certain sense makes accessible and con-creates. In the same way, two friends experience a greater freedom through their friendship, because it places in front of them a deeper and more effective way of accessing reality which, according to the Judaeo-Christian matrix, is precisely made up of a web of relationships. Paradoxically, when we embrace and hold each other, we are freer and more open.

And this also happened during the lock-down, thanks to communication tools. It is true that they can be used very badly, encouraging idolatry, because of the role that image plays in them. But they can also be used in the service of relationships. On the contrary, an extraordinary and paradoxical cognitive possibility opened up by the pandemic has been that of making people less lonely. In fact, before, loneliness was fought by trying to be with others as much as possible, but without ever really entering into a relationship with them. A person stayed in company in order not to feel lonely, but the price paid was very high, because he or she had to constantly meet the expectations of others. The fundamental problem was not "what do I desire?", "what do I think?", "what do I like to do?", but "what do they expect from me?" A somewhat harsh metaphor that can describe the society that originated from this approach is that of duty-free shops in the airport: wherever you flew, the products were either the same or very similar. Instead, identity, by definition, is difference, and a world that does not allow for differences is like an ecological disaster for relationships, which cannot develop and survive. But the separation, the confrontation with the real limit, even the radical one of death, with the consequent frustration, paradoxically have taught people that it is possible to survive without aperitifs, without new purchases, without football and sporting events, without a gym, without a health spa and without a thousand other things, that surely in time we would have tried to declare fundamental human rights. This has allowed that in returning to normality many people have been enriched by the ability to be alone, which paradoxically is the condition for not being alone. In fact, in company one can be immersed in the darkest solitude, if one is not also in relationship. But in order to be in relationship, one must be oneself and, therefore, know how to be in difference. The lock-down has decreased the ideal charge and expectations in personal relationships, allowing a more authentic and effective confrontation with reality.

6. The Fall of the (Post-Modern) Gods

This can produce the fall of post-modern idols. These have been described with great lucidity by Pierangelo Sequeri in a brief and incisive book that poses to the reader questions that, in light of what has emerged in and after the pandemic, appear as inescapable as they are urgent. The inexorable fall into fights, as in the Greek *polemos*, due to the loss of the *logos*, a regressive path with respect to the path that led to the Judaeo-Christian matrix, is traced with great lucidity, illustrating the process through four exemplary figures: the absolutization of youth (I), the obsession with growth (II), the totalitarianism of communication (III), and the irreligion of secularization (IV).[43] The review allows one to realize the dramatically dehumanizing scope of what Sequeri calls "the ethical autism of the sentimental ego."[44]

(I) The first idol is the narcissistic declination of eternal youth that reverses, as in the Greek and Babylonian myths, the relationship between fathers and sons. The imperative to remain young at all costs increasingly reduces the subject to a compulsive consumer who, like a new Kronos, begins to feed on his own offspring. The life that escapes is demanded of the following generations to whom it would be rightfully due. How many children are forced to live for the expectations of their parents, regardless of their political or cultural alignment. The cause and effect of all this is the disappear-

---

43   Cf. P. Sequeri, *Contro gli idoli postmoderni* (Torino: Lindau, 2012), p. 7.
44   Cf. *ibid.*, p. 8.

ance of initiation rites, because they imply a confrontation with limits and constitute a definitive passage. If everything must always remain in possibility, that is, in the ideal, then it cannot be defined. Even at the psychopathological level, more and more people are decompensating before the fundamental stages and inescapable passages of life: choosing university, finishing it, entering the job market, getting married. As the Italian theologian rightly observes, adolescence invades every age, both forward and backward, in a drift towards systemic narcissism that erases history, the seasons and the unity of life, depriving them of meaning.[45] What has disappeared is precisely the relationship, expunged from the post-modern cultural matrix together with the reference to the Trinitarian faith. In fact, personal history is one and different at the same time, as always happens in the development of a living being, a tree for example. The dimensions of binding (*religo*) and referring (*refero*) must be present at the same time, because what gives unity to growth coincides with the upward tendency. In the vegetal sphere the tendency to the beyond is only physical, necessary and finite. For the human being, on the other hand, the dimension of personal history is a consequence of creation in the image and likeness of the triune God. From this perspective, death itself is not the end, but the beginning, insofar as it is the end par excellence, which, however, in Christ reveals itself as the threshold. Instead, the post-modern cultural matrix offers a "bonsai life", in the extreme effort to remain always a flower, always a bud, without ever crossing any definitive and initiatory threshold that opens to life through difference. After all, the post-modern subject is trapped in a form of identity (*religo*) that denies every difference (*refero*), because of the symbolic killing of the father.

But how does the idol of the eternal child, the *puer aeternus*, the name Sequeri gives to this temptation to remain forever

45 Cf. *ibid.*, pp. 16 and 19.

juvenile, fare in the pandemic? In fact, the ongoing frustration at the mismatch between the ideal and the real has clashed, in some cases for the first time, with a deeply real and concrete frustration. Being forced to live with one's family or having to be alone in isolation has shattered one's own and others' expectations. The inescapable threshold of death entered our homes through the images on the television. The uncertainty of the future has brought attention to what *is*, as opposed to what *could be*, in the most basic sense of what's in the fridge, what's in the house, what's in me and so on. Of course, not everyone reacted the same way. Someone saw their neighbors' faces for the first time, looking out of the window for a breath of fresh air; others left a note with their cell phones for the elderly, offering to go shopping for them. Some extolled doctors and nurses as heroes, others complained if they lived in their building, for fear of contagion. But in any case, no one was able to escape the confrontation with a danger and a decision, with respect to themselves and with respect to others. The mask itself hides the face, subtracting surface from the aesthetic game, but implies awareness of the inescapable relationship with the other. Perhaps we have the opportunity to reread the lock-down, the pandemic and what followed them, as an initiation on a planetary scale, which can allow us to recover ground with respect to the dehumanization operated by the idol, which reduces the being to an ideal image.

(II) This is immediately connected with the second example presented by Sequeri: growth without limit. In fact, this postmodern divinity is inseparable from the first, being its translation on the social level. The genealogy here is difficult to reconstruct, unlike in ancient myths. Defining whether eternal youth or limitless progress comes first would be like trying to decide whether the chicken or the egg came first. Sequeri identifies, with almost ferocious clarity, the link with the adolescent dimension, along with the pathology that accompanies it on the social level: the temptation put into play by this idol is not pleasure as such, but the mere mental possibility of pleasure itself. The power that seduces here is that of the availability of the object: "enjoyment of available enjoyment" that necessarily leads to impotence.[46] As can be immediately grasped, this is a second-order idol, in the sense that it does not simply work to disfigure the real, but attacks the very conditions of the relationship with reality itself. In other words, if I like wine, I am exposed to the temptation of drinking too much of it, but this causes a hangover that in some way gives me back an element of reality about my mistake, about the fact that the road travelled in search of the infinite that my heart asks for has been barred by the finitude of the object sought. With this idol, on the other hand, we are not talking about drinking too much, but about having hectoliters of wine that one could drink, but never does, very expensive unopened bottles that one is pleased with. It is like having many books and never reading them, stopping to contemplate them in the bookcase. To avoid frustration, enjoyment is virtualized. And this is exacerbated by the idolatrous capacity of money, which can potentially take any form that our imagination wants to give it. Thanks to it, consumerism breaks through the emotional dimension, invading the space of the search for meaning in everyday life. It is now clear that in many cases, when we go out to buy something or when we order an item on the internet, what is at stake is not only the object of which we may have more or less need, but even more deeply the emotion of the new, of the conquest.

On this idol, the pandemic has struck with ferocity, catching everyone off guard. If before it the various countries and companies were struggling to offer tenths of a percentage more in GDP or in dividends and share prices, suddenly the losses were counted in tens of percentage points. This socio-economic "desert" has laid

46 Cf. *ibid.*, p. 39.

bare the central node induced by the contemporary cultural matrix: Is the economy or the human being first? Which is the end and which the means? The dogma of unlimited growth has begun to wobble in the face of a question that even a child could ask: Why grow? Or rather, for whom to grow? We were told that there were too many of us and that the planet could not sustain us all, but at the same time we are told that the only way to "get along well" is to consume more and more. How is this possible? The ecological question itself enters into this game, including its anthropological dimension. The illusion that it was enough to consume to be happy collapsed under the judgment of the energy limit, thanks to which the question of the end re-emerges after the modern universal reduction of everything to a means. On the other hand, the term economy itself refers to the law (*nomos*) of the home (*oikia*) and the home is always someone's home, that is, it presupposes a family and relationships. And also ecology refers to the home, being the *logos* of the *oikia*. Indeed, the present situation can be a great opportunity to recognize that economic mechanisms are not necessitating determinisms, as if they were an inexorable post-modern fate, but are the result of choices made by human beings, who exercise their freedom, not only on a macro level, but also on a micro level. The critical value, in the positive sense, of this testing period can be grasped by thinking about what we sought and bought during the lock-down. Re-reading based on the Judeo-Christian matrix subjects growth to the judgment of relationship, which like a plant or a puppy, requires time and waste, to have real gain and enjoyment then.

(III) Also linked to the idol of growth as a virtualization of enjoyment is the idol of communication which, starting from the idealist ontologizing of the Cartesian *cogito*, begins to be identified with being itself. The commandment of this divinity is: "You are as you appear, you are if you appear". The question is no longer merely economic, but one of identity. When passers-by, instead of rescuing accident victims, stop to take selfies, not to sell pictures to newspapers but to get likes, they are behaving inhumanly. In a way, such behaviors are sacrifices to this divinity that swallows up its believers, digesting them in a media stream that is purely functional and an end in itself.

Precisely in the context of the pandemic, a terrifying example of this process is the case of Maatje Benassi, a US Army reservist who had attended the Military World Games in Wuhan in October 2019. An American conspiracy theorist posted a video on *YouTube* pointing to Benassi as case zero of the Covid outbreak and the news was amplified by Chinese algorithms to support the narrative of contagion brought from the US to China. In truth, the woman never contracted Covid, though her life was destroyed by this "cyber" epidemic, with no recourse against *YouTube*.

The perverse communicative effect is also due to the role of algorithms driving the social media mechanism. Like a new deity, real victims fall on the altar of new sacrificial forms. As the story of Justine Sacco shows. In 2013, she was a 30-year-old head of communications for a digital media company who, first in New York and then in London while waiting for her flight back to South Africa, posted a message on Twitter joking about her return to Africa and the risks of contracting AIDS. When she put her mobile phone in flight mode before her 11-hour flight, she could not have suspected that, starting with some of her 170 followers, those few dozen characters of hers would be transformed into the number one trending topic by the algorithms that amplify the polarization of opinions, causing her to lose her job and irreparable damage to her fame, which she only realized once she had landed.

These examples show that human relations cannot become objects of commerce and exchange without hurting personal dignity itself and poisoning the communicative habitat. In social media, the product is users' relationships. These very useful tools risk being transformed into companies which own the words and forms of

expression that people use to communicate. But language, by definition, is a relational asset that cannot be owned by anyone, except
at the price of dehumanising the users themselves, depriving them
of a fundamental element of their dignity. If this happens, one has
fallen into a terrible (even demonic) temptation.

Always at some point in life or in a significant activity the idol
appears and asks us for our soul. That is our "desert", the insurmountable boundary of the human, beyond which we are not the
ones communicating, but we begin to be communicated, we are
not the ones using, but we are used. This is the ruinous fall from
subject to object, an abyss that attracts with an almost invincible
force, because it deprives us of responsibility. As with the force of
gravity, we tell ourselves that we can do nothing but fall. And then
we complain because we feel alone and inadequate. But how is it
possible to be recognized and loved in our uniqueness if all our efforts are dedicated to conforming to categories, to images that are
foreign to us?

The media system simply has to sell, so that the important
thing is no longer what is true and what is not true, but what creates an audience or earns views and likes. From this point of view,
as I have learned from direct experience in years of radio broadcasting, in such a setting dialectics is the very purpose of the media
act, because it attracts and binds both those of one faction and
those of the other. Everything must tend to produce a Superbowl
atmosphere, so that as many people as possible listen to the advertising messages. But this still belongs to the domain of the idol of
limitless growth. What is produced by communication elevated to
idol status is that the very identity of the person is colonized by
the parasite of media recognition. The lack of real and founding
relationships exposes people to this spasmodic search for virtual
and ephemeral relationships. This is possible because the dimension of the *refero* refers to the symbolic sphere, in which the human
being is ontologically dropped. The idol takes possession of this

sphere and depowers it, folding it back on itself, in such a way that an entire society becomes like the fool who, when the wise man points to the moon, looks at the finger. Even worse, here we risk becoming like the dog who, when the master points to the food, looks at his hand. This example highlights the dehumanizing element of a communication that symbolically folds back on itself. In fact, the distinctive cognitive characteristic of the human being compared to primates is metacognition, defined as the ability to recognize the other as an intentionally knowing subject. Babies develop metacognition around the age of nine months, and it is the basis of language and culture. In the herds of gorillas or chimpanzees, in fact, sometimes a member discovers a tool or an effective method for subsistence, but this discovery dies with this member, because it does not have the ability to teach the novelty to another.[47] In other words, the communicative environment in which we are immersed, by reducing the capacity for metacognition and passivating the subject, acts in an anti-evolutionary sense.

This has effects on the inner world of the human being, who is increasingly dependent on external stimuli. The perception of loneliness and the lack of meaning are anesthetized through the continuous use of sounds or images, which stimulate the subject from the outside. Emotional life thus becomes totally dependent on communicative consumerism. When the stimulus is absent, the person finds herself in an untenable situation, since her inner world is shrunken. Because of this, she cannot make memories or relive emotions, which she has entirely externalized. It is as if her identity has passed into the cloud.[48]

This recalls the relevance of the myth of Theuth, narrated by

47 Cf. M. Tomasello, *Origins of Human Communication* (Cambridge, MA: MIT Press, 2008).

48 Cf. S. Turkle, *Alone Together: Why We Expect More from Technology and Less from Each Other* (New York: Basic Books, 2012).

Plato in the *Phaedrus*.[49] Here Socrates recounts that the Egyptian deity who gives the myth its name came to the Egyptian king Thamus and offered him the gift of the writing he had invented. The king refused this gift, because it would have led the people to forgetfulness and, therefore, ignorance. In fact, thanks to writing, they would have ceased to remember from within, to rely on an external medium.

Digitisation and social media are a further revolution in relation to the transition from oral to print-based culture, the impact of which was highlighted with great clarity by Marshall McLuhan.[50] Now the risk is even greater because not only the intellectual and cultural world, but also the relational and emotional world is being externalised. But, at this juncture, the lock-downs represented an opportunity. Just think of the confrontation with silence. Suddenly, communication possibilities have been drastically reduced. Although in theory the show must go on, in practice the show has stopped. The media act has begun to be exercised from the domestic dimension, with even amusing results, such as the child who enters the frame during a live broadcast of his journalist father. Ambivalence is, of course, always present, because in some cases daily communication has invaded existential zones that were previously explored only by reality shows. Soon we were saved by virtual backgrounds, which made up for when a nice library was not available. Even people less accustomed to the camera had to learn how to improve webcam shots. But the central point is that the mechanism of spectacularization has jammed. If the protagonists of talk-shows became doctors and virologists, it is clear that disease and death were in the foreground.

In a certain sense a purification from idolatry was triggered,

49 Plato, *Phaedrus*, 274c–275b.
50 M. McLuhan, *The Gutenberg Galaxy: The Making of Typographic Man* (Toronto: University of Toronto Press, 1962).

because it was no longer possible to anesthetize oneself and not think about the limit. The tension towards the infinite of the human heart clashed violently against the walls of the houses, the real and daily relationships with one's neighbor and only the neighbor, the impossibility of going to the hairdresser, or the recourse to remote working that undermined the recreational and playful dimension of the media. Television series, after the initial binge, began to tire, contradicting Reed Hastings, the CEO of Netflix, who on 18 April 2017 had presented sleep as his company's only real competitor. On the positive side, psychiatrists started following their patients online, from their own homes, finding a greater closeness to them, as if the shared consciousness of being exposed to mortal danger was gently bringing them down from their pedestal, opening up new possibilities for treatment. Or, in virtual meetings it proved much more difficult to argue, because everything was recorded and one could see one's face comically distorted by anger. But above all, it is absolutely generalized experience that all students, of all levels, have grasped that school or university is not only the information received, which even during the lockdown has passed through the media, but above all it is the relationships between people. All, without exception, have decreed that face-to-face teaching is better. This result is extremely significant, because it can help an entire generation to bring the media back to what is its function, that is, to be a means and not ends.

(IV) The spiritual root of the idol constituted by the totalitarization of communication is profoundly theological, because it leans in a parasitic form precisely on that creation in the image and likeness of God which constitutes the human being. The violence inherent in the operation consists in emptying from within the relational content of the image itself, narcissistically folding it back on itself. In order to escape the mortal enigma that the idol poses to us, as the pythia of Delphi sacred to Apollo posed to Oedipus, we must ask ourselves: But if we are not in the image of God, in the image of who are we? Or worse, of what? The last example given by Pierangelo Sequeri reveals precisely this theological root: The fiercest idol is secularization, not understood as a positive affirmation of the value of the secular dimension with respect to the failure of the religious institution to respect its autonomy, but secularization as the definitive overcoming of the religious question itself. This is the extreme outcome of a certain drift of post-modernism that abandons even the dialectic of Marx's Prometheus and the unbridled passion of Nietzsche's Dionysus to place itself under the aegis of Narcissus.[51] Here, Sequeri explains, "there is no modern confrontation with the law of the father, but there is post-modern regression to the womb of the mother. Prometheus is rebellious towards the divine, but at least he accepts to sacrifice himself in favor of humans. Narcissus is indifferent to the divine and the human."[52] The dehumanizing totalitarianism of this overcoming of the dialectic had been prophetically sensed by Aldous Huxley, who in *Brave New World*, a novel published in 1932, before the consequences of the tragic dictatorial experiences of the twentieth century based on violence became visible, had already illustrated a further stage in the transition to a dictatorship based on enjoyment, in which consciousnesses submitted voluntarily and not by force. The inhuman outcome and the unsustainability of such a perspective emerge with great dramatic force in the narrative.

Here the theological and the sociological analysis converge decisively, because the denial of the Trinitarian matrix, i.e. the relational one, of society generates monsters. Moreover, in the myth, Narcissus dies. The example of Oedipus' Thebes shows how the simple blurring of relational distinctions risks collapsing social life. It is no wonder, then, that tragedy is inevitable when relationship is denied *a priori* by withdrawal into oneself. A terrible joke that

51   Cf. Sequeri, *Contro gli idoli postmoderni*, p. 74.
52   *Ibid.*, p. 77.

has been going around in this period imagines the dialogue between a couple, in which the woman says, "At least during the lockdown we could see each other in video-calls" and the man replies "Actually, I was always looking at myself". Relationship in the proper sense is not possible with Narcissus, so the foundation of society is non-existent.

This outcome is the result of a cultural matrix that intentionally and knowingly denies the triune God to give itself to idols, post-modern and ancient. The consequence can be no other than war. Neil Gaiman's novel from 2001 entitled *American Gods*,[53] from which a television series was also taken, tells of the clash between Odin, in the guise of a kind of mafia boss, followed by some primitive gods, and the new gods, which are the media, television, internet and so on. At the end, it turns out that the clash was actually desired and provoked by Odin himself, who needed victims, sacrifices in his name. Idolatry is always the same and always leads to the same result. To erase God from culture does not mean to get rid of the sense of guilt, but to fall under the dominion of new and ancient idols. So the health crisis and what followed it have removed the illusion that death is a theory and it has made us touch the reality of loneliness beyond any social illusion. For this reason, the next step of the proposed path dwells on the link between secularization and the cultural matrix of society.

53 N. Gaiman, *American Gods* (New York: HarperCollins, 2001).

7. The Return of Religion

The confrontation with this last idol should make us reflect, because after having lived through difficult moments, the consequences of which have also remained as wounds and painful traces in the psyche, people now have an open question. If post-modern idols waver, the possibility of rediscovering the Judeo-Christian matrix is real and concrete. The pretended modern self- sufficiency has been shattered and the narcissistic totalitarianism of post-modernity is following the same destiny. The clash with the limit has opened up the possibility of a real relationship with the other and, therefore, of authentic freedom and sociality. We are facing an epochal turning point that is an opportunity for transcendence.

But in order to seize this opportunity, Christian thought must become aware of the treasure it holds. In fact, the demand for salvation is the natural condition for the precious pearl and the treasure in the field to be recognized. Only those who know they are sick seek the cure. Instead, the danger of idolatry has long since ceased to be discussed, even within the church. Salvation has gone out of the semantic horizon of preaching, as if a doctor would no longer talk about diseases, because "it looks bad", or a plumber would be ashamed to communicate that he can repair broken toilets. A scathing metaphor might liken today's believers to hostesses or stewards on airplanes who explain safety rules before takeoff, without being heard by anyone. Christian thinkers themselves run the risk of being perceived as custodians of a museum, constantly confronted with beautiful realities, whose salvific content has, however, been forgotten. And in the first place, perhaps, they themselves have become accustomed to so much beauty and truth. Here we are not only referring to the tendency to return to God described by the ana-theism proposed by Richard Kearney.[54] The issue is more radical, as it is linked to the essential role of spirituality for mankind.

Post-modern polytheism, in fact, is only in appearance open and relativistic, like the Olympus of the Romans. The Christian martyrs show that any position could find a place in it except criticism of idols. Already with the death of Socrates the question of the relationship between politics and religion had been posed in dramatic terms. The world dominated by idols is neither free nor human, so much so that the very success of early Christianity in the Roman empire was due not to any sort of power, alliance, or connivance, but to the humanity of which it was the bearer. Is it really enough to abandon the Mosaic distinction, hence the Judeo-Christian matrix's claim to truth, as Jan Assmann argues,[55] to avoid violence? Is the One really the reason for intolerance, as Peter Sloterdijk claims?[56] It seems to me that it is enough to read the news, follow the social networks or go to the stadium, to grasp that the solution to the human dialectic cannot be so easy. And the war after the pandemic confirms this conclusion.

We have seen that the Bible recognizes a transcendent One as the origin and source of the world's immanent relationality. Human beings carry within themselves the trace of this transcendence in the impossibility of satisfying their desire from within the finite dimension. Beginning with Adam and Eve after sin, and

---

54 R. Kearney, *Anatheism: Returning to God after God* (New York: Columbia University Press, 2011).

55 J. Assmann, *Of God and Gods: Egypt, Israel, and the Rise of Monotheism* (Madison, WI: University of Wisconsin Press, 2008).

56 P. Sloterdijk, *God's Zeal: The Battle of the Three Monotheisms* (Cambridge, UK: Polity Press, 2009).

then with Cain and Abel, the other becomes a symbol of this dissatisfaction. But only because one looks at the world and oneself apart from one's relationship with the Father. Herein lies the point. A society that eliminates the transcendent reference to God remains a slave to wars between the gods. The ancient myths and Greek tragedies are there to warn us. But even the terrible experiences of the last century remind us of what happens when the Judeo-Christian matrix is secularized. The essential point is that polytheism is violent because it is closed, as it places the idea above reality, segregating its followers in the limited, where there is no other possibility but to compete endlessly in the useless and desperate attempt to relieve their thirst for infinity. Prometheus becomes Sisyphus.

If polytheistic societies stood, it was only because of sacrifices, as René Girard has shown. He moves, initially, from Darwinist positions and, leaning on some of Freud's results, extends the evolutionist conception to the cultural sphere.[57] Its purpose is to counter religious relativism, the result of rationalist anthropological analysis of the last two centuries. Key to his perspective is violence and its relationship with religion mediated by the mimetic dimension of desire. He starts from the observation that both humans and animals tend to copy each other's desires: We compete for the females of the pack, for food, etc. It is enough for someone to look to one side and all turn their gaze in the same direction. At the base of this is metacognition, the foundation of language and culture. But, as we have said, while among animals competition generally stops before producing the death of one of the contenders, among humans it is not so and it can be reproduced indefinitely, according to the perverse logic of revenge. In contrast to Freud's sexual reductionism, Girard extends the object of possible conflict, tracing

57 Cf. R. Girard, *Wissenschaft und christlicher Glaube* (Tübingen: Mohr Siebeck, 2007), p. 18.

the emergence of religious prohibitions precisely to the need to stop the spread of violence and to preserve life. He even goes so far as to identify the moment of hominization with the emergence of these religious prohibitions. The surprising result is that institutions and culture would be essentially religious in nature.

The myths narrate this process and this is the reason for the numerous parallels between them, such as the presence of an epidemic, of a monstrous being and of sacrifices, caught by the rationalist and historicist studies of the nineteenth century, which concluded with the reduction of Christianity to a myth among others. At the basis of these parallels there is an anthropological constant, which the Judeo-Christian matrix recognizes precisely in the creation of the image and likeness of God. Thus, the solution to the violent crisis was obtained by converging violence on a scapegoat, according to an evolutionarily convenient solution, because it sacrifices the one to make the many live. This is the same situation in which Oedipus, Antigone and Socrates, in their individuality, are victims of the universal. The mimetic malaise would appear in the myths as a reference to an epidemic and the focus on a single individual of the group, perhaps marked by positive or negative peculiarities, such as being beautiful, a king, a foreigner, crippled or blind, restores peace to the community. The victim of the lynching would then be deified precisely because he or she is attributed this miraculous return of calm. C.S. Lewis' novel *Till We Have Faces: A Myth Retold*,[58] dedicated to a reinterpretation of the pagan myth of Cupid and Psyche in the light of Christian revelation, perfectly illustrates the mechanism of human sacrifice and the consequent deification of the victims. This was the foundation of ancient civil religion, both for the *polis* and for Rome, as the founding fratricide of Remus by Romulus reveals, which explains

58 Cf. C.S. Lewis, *Till We Have Faces: A Myth Retold* (London: Geoffrey Bles, 1956).

why the crimes of the gods are always so human. Girard's theory is, therefore, a radical critique of the social contract.[59]

This has a deep cognitive implication, because the mechanism would be possible precisely as it is unconscious. The lynchers, in fact, never doubt the guilt of the victims, but they always act unanimously, and the mythological narratives faithfully reflect this clear and distinct judgment. The ritual would arise, then, from the need to reproduce in a less violent way the solution to the crisis induced by the mimetic mechanism, which necessarily recharges, threatening peace. The effect would be obtained through a symbolic substitution of the victim, in a process similar to the catharsis attributed by Aristotle to Greek tragedy.

Faced with the modern observer convinced of the common conclusion, according to Nietzsche's genealogical approach, that religions would be nothing more than a human invention,[60] the French thinker highlights the positive value for the subsistence of humanity of religious prohibitions and sacrifices. For him, the essence of culture would be religious and could not be eliminated, on pain of the end of mankind. This is anything but a remote possibility precisely because the human being is not only a biological being, but also cultural, that is symbolic. The double structure of binding (*religo*) and referring (*refero*) founds human existence in relationality. But the modern reading is not able to grasp the radical difference between primitive religions and Christianity. The cross of Christ is read as the lynching of a scapegoat, which would have suffered in Jerusalem the same fate that struck Oedipus in Thebes. Celsus already in the second century AD had noted this parallelism and today it is common to think, sometimes even among people of Christian tradition, that Christianity is a religion like the others, which is imposed only by the alliance with the imperial power, and as such can be overcome.

59   Cf. Girard, *Wissenschaft und christlicher Glaube*, p. 22.
60   Cf. *ibid.*, p. 36.

But it is precisely here that Girard's reflection shows all its force, since he proves that Christ can in no way be considered a deified scapegoat. In fact, simultaneously with the awareness of the similarities between the Cross and the pagan sacrifices, radical differences also emerge: the Gospel is a literary *unicum*, because it affirms that Christ is innocent and in it the unconsciousness typical of mythical narratives is absent. Moreover, there is no unanimity of the crowd, since Christ is said to be innocent by a minority, presented in all its human frailty, as the betrayal of the apostles reveals, but which for this very reason testifies to a reality beyond human capacity. The myths agree with the lynchers, the Gospels do not. The myth does not see the innocence of Oedipus, the Gospel reveals the innocence of Christ, and along with His innocence, that of Oedipus as well. In doing so, the mechanism of violent mimesis comes to light. Jesus, with his voluntary death, blows away the veil that covered the sacrifice of the scapegoat, revealing the innocence of all the victims in history, starting with Abel.

The Gospel narratives are extremely realistic, so much so that Peter himself at the moment of his betrayal is portrayed facing the temptation of being absorbed by the crowd that condemns his Lord and can only resist through the gaze of Christ and the power of the Holy Spirit, the Paraclete, that is, the defender of the victims, who achieves an enlightenment incomparably superior to that of Voltaire and Rousseau.[61]

Girard highlights the absolute singularity of this revelation: only in Judaism had the possibility that the victims were innocent appeared before Christ. Indeed, many times in the Bible the violent mob is condemned, while the individual victim is rehabilitated. By taking for granted the gains made possible by the Judeo-Christian matrix, we have lost the ability to notice the uniqueness, compared to other ancient narratives, of Joseph, who forgives his

61   Cf. *ibid.*, p. 52–56.

brothers after twice becoming a scapegoat; of Job in the face of his friends and wife who are like the mob of an incipient lynching; of the Suffering Servant and the Psalms, which embarrass us with the praying man's demand for revenge, but which we no longer recognize as absolute novelty. No other text had given voice to the innocence of the victim.

From this point of view, it is essential that it is the Gospel itself that presents Christ as the scapegoat with the phrase "it is better that one man should die."[62] The expression Lamb of God is at the beginning of all four Gospels and is the gentlest synonym for scapegoat. So Jesus fulfills the role of a mythical scapegoat, but with the essential difference, compared to pagan sacrifices, that He does it freely by choice and precisely to blow up the perverse mechanism of violence that always tends to reproduce itself. This is why Christ applies to Himself the verse of the psalm: "They hated me for no reason".[63]

This shows that the alternative to the Judeo-Christian matrix is not easy, because one must reckon with the violence of sacrifices and idols. Post-modern relativism exacerbates the possibilities of conflict, for the means at its disposal to narcissistically fold minds and souls are mighty. Post-modern idols are stronger. The best minds of humanity are dedicated to financialization, which can offer the human imagination any good because of money's ability to be converted into different goods; advertising, which constantly manipulates human desire by attracting it to ever new products; and virtualization, which systematically works to replace real relationships with digital ones. The new boundary is post-humanism. Video games become "meta-verse", in the sense of presenting themselves as alternative worlds where people can get married, as happened to a couple during the lock-down, or organize social events, concerts, conferences. The mechanism works, but it also has a perverse dimension that in the

62   John 18:14.
63   Psalm 35:19.

long run produces depression, dissociation, anorexia and bulimia, because one cannot play around with human desire, that is, with the ultimate bottom of our heart, with impunity. This situation generates pathologies in an infallible manner—monotonous and unvarying—thus making it possible to profit from the pathologies themselves, as in the case of drug trafficking. Paradoxically, this has metaphysical and theological roots because man's infinite desire, confronted with the disappointment in the finiteness of the things he manages to obtain, compulsively seeks a new promise of fulfillment, which in constant reiteration generates addiction and dehumanization. . But at a certain point the human can't stand it, the psyche tears itself apart. A society of pushers is not possible. Indeed, if one has some unsatisfied desire, some hunger at least, one can hope that by struggling to obtain the desired object one will be happy. But if one has already tried everything, one necessarily ends up in meaninglessness.

Girard's is one of the harshest critiques of post-modernism and offers one of the most effective representations of the psychopathological double-bind that characterizes modernity. This can be summarized in the injunction "you have to be yourself alone", or "you have to be free without relationships", or "you have to be unique by being anything".[64] The confrontation with Gianni Vattimo on the violent nature of relativism is one of the most valuable contributions of Girard, because it highlights how behind "weak thought" lies precisely the return of idols and polytheistic totalitarianism.[65] The relational perspective allows to show how the double-bind described corresponds to a pathology not only psychic, but first of all metaphysical, because human desire is ontologically constituted by the relationship with the transcendent dimension,

64 Cf. G. Fornari, *Dionysus, Christ, and the Death of God* (East Lansing, MI: Michigan State University Press, 2020).

65 Cf. R. Girard-G. Vattimo, *Christianity, Truth, and Weak Faith* (New York: Columbia University Press, 2009).

which protects from the binary reductionism that leads to the narcissistic prison. Girard points out, even in his literary analysis,[66] that romantic idealism can be redeemed only by the truth of the novel, in which the Trinitarian dimension of human desire is recovered, giving back citizenship to its excess.

This requires, however, that difference be recognized, along with identity, as a co-constitutive element of the real, an affirmation that in the Judeo-Christian matrix is not contradictory because that God who creates in His image and likeness is one and triune, so it carries within Himself the relational distinction.

But pre-virus Western society was built in a post-modern key on the denial of differences for fear of conflict. This was a consequence and development of the modern killing of the father, which led to a true generalized slavery, as is always the case when dealing with idols. In fact, the true God makes one live because He gives life, while idols take it away. Western consumerist society has been built on mimetic desire, systematically against the ninth and tenth commandments. And the discourse here is not moral, but purely phenomenological: If the only way of "salvation" is consumption, then we must necessarily permit ourselves to be continually seduced, allowing the tension towards infinity that characterizes our desire to be "secularized", that is, horizontally bound to the rock of the finite, like Prometheus. The eagle continues to gnaw at our liver, with no hope of redemption. This led to the crisis described by René Girard, that is, to the collapse of the Trinitarian dimension of human desire, which is instead based on the vertical transcendent direction. From here originated a real pathoplastic society, whose limit is immediately evident from the relational perspective: For the human being it is, in fact, impossible to be himself alone,

66   Cfr. F. Bergamino, *René Girard: La res svelata dalla letteratura*, in *Alice dietro lo specchio. Letteratura e conoscenza della realtà*, F. Bergamino (ed.), (Roma: Edizioni Sabinae, 2013), pp. 121–158.

because he is ontologically creature and son and, as such, has his identity in the relationship with his origin and his brothers. The naivety of the French Revolution was to invoke freedom, equality and fraternity, symbolically going against the father. But how can we be brothers without being children of the same father?

And yet, this can also be the starting point for an awareness of the need to rediscover the message of religion and spirituality in general, or at least to bring the comparison to the most authentic level of the cultural matrix of reference. The pandemic has accelerated a process that was already underway, undermining the consumerist and globalist illusion of being able to avoid all limits. The various dimensions of this desert, from physical silence to the impossibility of moving and traveling freely as before, up to the scandalous extreme of a little more poverty in this opulent West, are occasions to rediscover, beyond one's own faith, that the human being lives of and in relationship. In fact, as we have seen, human relationship constitutively presupposes the encounter with a limit, because the confrontation with the beyond is inescapable. But this refers back to a religious question. And in this health crisis, the epiphany of the relationship has brought out that dimension of the Judeo-Christian matrix which is Trinitarian ontology.[67] It consists in the awareness that the one and triune God is the origin of being and that, therefore, can offer light even to those who do not believe, but are not satisfied by a merely substantialist position, which does not recognize cultural multiplicity, and therefore communion, as co-principle of reality. This perspective allows us to reread the limit itself as a threshold, a passage (as in Passover, the Jewish term for Easter) towards a beyond that is radically *Other* with a capital letter. This founds the relationship of every human being with the (lower case) *other* and, therefore, his or her relational

67 Cf. P. Coda, "L'ontologia trinitaria: cos'e`?" in *Sophia* 4 (2012): pp. 159–179.

identity, for which one cannot be oneself alone. As pointed out in the critique of post-modern idols, the consequences are terribly concrete. Before, we thought we were immersed in relationships, but we were alone, precisely because of our inability to stand in difference and the frustration it causes by clashing with our infinite desire. The difficulty in living together in marriage demonstrates this, with the consequent crisis of the family, in which the parent-child relationships even present an inversion. The former have begun to conceive of the latter as projections of themselves, charging them with the responsibility of satisfying their parents' infinite desire. But being left alone during the lock-down, with one's relatives or without, has forced one to stay in real frustration, which now allows a relational flowering, because the confrontation with the limit can play the function of initiation that makes one capable of being oneself with others. More radically still, the illusion of not being mortal has fallen and the consciousness of the limit has not only made us closer, but also conscious of the need for salvation, a reality that makes religion meaningful. And this has political-economic consequences as well.

8. The Fall of "Another" Wall

With the fall of the Berlin Wall in 1989, it seemed that liberalism had definitively defeated communism. Globalization, consumerism and financialization were presented as irreversible phenomena. Economic life consisted in a continuous and frenzied competition to multiply profits or attract investments, which Girard's analysis allows us to read in an idolatrous sense. But thirty years later, suddenly, a pandemic shut down the whole world. The question was no longer how much space emerging economies would gain and where investors would decide to take their capital, but everyone found themselves with their machines stopped and in deficit. The economic declination of the double-bind mentioned above went into crisis, the noose was broken, because the absolute dogma of consumption at any cost was "judged" in the desert of the real economy, here understood in the most fundamental sense of what the human being needs to live. Suddenly, the virus re-aligned the economy with this dimension. Only those who had savings were able to survive the lean times. Thus the closure has forced individuals to realize their responsibility as buyers, becoming more conscious and reinterpreting their needs starting from real relationships and not imaginary ones, while at the same time undermining the dogma of consumerism.

It seems as if the pandemic has brought down a second "Berlin Wall": If the one to the East had fallen, now the one to the West seems to be collapsing. More properly, we must recognize that it is the same wall, as we are simply faced with the continuous fall of idols, which always marks history. The wall that physically enclosed us in a world of collectivist imposition is not different from the one that culturally imprisons us in an individualist conception of the human being. The political implications of what has been said are evident, because the ability to manipulate developed to push consumption, exploiting in a parasitic way the need for transcendence and relations of the human being, has become an irreplaceable element of the real democratic confrontation. But high consumption eventually has to confront the energy limit and this leads to conflict, as the period following the pandemic shows. From this point of view, modern democracy itself was already on the verge of a deep crisis. In fact, without care for the family and education, it becomes show-business, with the current aggravating factor of the passage from the sphere of television to that of the world of social networks.

Essentially, simplifying but trying to present the heart of the matter, both economics and politics are structured in a manipulative sense. If the price of products is totally unrelated to reality, then the ideal customer becomes the drug addict, who is willing to pay any price for a dose. This is why mafias thrive on drug trafficking, gambling and prostitution, all of which are addictive. And this also seems to have become the business paradigm for legitimate activities. But the problem is that manipulation causes damage to the people who suffer it, because it hurts their dignity, which is based on the very freedom that the liberal state champions. At the democratic level the discourse is similar, also because the connection between economy and politics is deep and inevitable. The idol of communication, after having placed communication itself above the relational dimension, with its consequent transition from means to end, thanks to the work of the idol of secularization, invades the political discussion, which ceases to be a dialogue between people, mediated by intermediary bodies, to become a media theater, where the winner is the one who shouts more or who better exploits the algorithms of search engines. It is not denied that communicative technique must be present in political confrontation. This has been the case since Athens, with the conflict between the Sophists and Socrates. Little by little we have moved from the supporters of the popular parties, who spent the nights before elections covering the posters of their opponents, to commercial television, up to social networks and computer platforms. What is contested here is that all this is reduced to a manipulative technique without any reference to the relational dimension, which should be the foundation of politics. Think of the *Facebook* and *Cambridge Analytica* scandal, where, regardless of how the facts unfolded, a new level of manipulation made possible by big data on the psychopolitical front clearly emerged.

In fact, when in 2014, Aleksandr Kogan, a professor at Cambridge University developed an app (called TIDYL = "This is Your Digital Life") to study the personality traits of its users, perhaps no one could have imagined that, thanks to a collaboration that began on June 4, 2014 with the political consulting firm *Cambridge Analytica*, data mining, data brokerage, and data analysis would bring psychopolitics to the world stage for the first time. In fact, not only those who had voluntarily run the personality test on TIDYL, but also their *Facebook* friends were unknowingly profiled. In this way, the number of those involved had already reached the level of several million in December 2015, when *The Guardian* revealed the collaboration between *Cambridge Analytica* and Ted Cruz, to be estimated at 87 million after the revelations of whistle-blower Christopher Wylie in March 2018. This led to a change in Facebook's privacy policy and Zuckerberg's hearing in the US Congress and the European Parliament.[68] The risks to democracy

68 This has introduced novelties to the very way journalism is done, see Cf. T. Venturini – R. Rogers, "'API-Based Research' or How can Digital Sociology and Journalism Studies Learn from the Facebook and Cambridge Analytica Data Breach," in *Digital Journalism*, 7 (2019), 532–540.

are obvious, as are the ethical questions that data mining opens up. What, then, is the metaphysical value of big data? To whom does this data belong and, above all, is it possible for people's relationships to become private property, exploited by a company or used to dope a democracy?

So the drive to consume is doubly manipulative because, on the one hand, it creates needs by parasitically exploiting the infinite desire of the human heart, but on the other hand it leads to consumer debt, eliminating that defense which is family savings. Thus, during the health crisis and the consequent economic-social destabilization, those who could not count on such a defense suffered heavily, risking not having the means for minimum subsistence. In the end, it is always a question of the modern double-bind, which the pandemic has revealed, making possible that judgment to which we are called. This is also reflected in the convergence of West and East: The individualist matrix, which finds one of its greatest realizations in the USA but which also has strong reflections in Europe, led to the rejection of the mask, as if wearing it to preserve oneself and others implied a loss of freedom, because after all it sees the relationship from the perspective of the one placed in dialectic with respect to the many. But this result is not so different from the collectivist matrix of consumerist China, where the mask is imposed by law under severe penalties, to the extreme of depriving personal freedoms, placing the many dialectically above the one, as in ancient sacrificial mechanisms.

The question is not, therefore, whether one is right or left, nor is it an issue of finding the right combination of different elements, as in the interesting attempts of Red Tories and Blue Labours. It all radically depends, instead, on the cultural matrix with which one works and on relations. So we can find the paradox that a country characterized by huge differences between economic classes has a "proletariat", but this is not able to trigger a communist revolution, because it lacks an educated middle class which can make judgments, because its very being in the "middle" makes it possible to perceive the difference between the two extremes. Therefore, paradoxically, where the economic system reduces social differences, a dialectical reaction can be produced. Similarly, the liberal state has lived off its inheritance thanks to the Christian tradition that has set the conditions for its birth. But now all the cultural capital has been burned and the risk is dehumanization induced by the manipulative system. Idols are implacable if the religious and spiritual dimension does not make it possible to deal with them. From this point of view, the pandemic can be read as an experimental proof of what Ernst-Wolfgang Böckenförde had formulated in 1967 through the homonymous dilemma, to which Pierangelo Sequeri himself refers:[69] "The liberal, secularized state is sustained by conditions it cannot itself guarantee. That is the great gamble it has made for the sake of liberty. On the one hand, as a liberal state it can only survive if the freedom it grants to its citizens is regulated from within, out of the moral substance of the individual and the homogeneity of society. On the other hand, it cannot seek to guarantee these inner regulatory forces by its own efforts—that is to say, with the instruments of legal coercion and authoritative command—without abandoning its liberalness, and relapsing, on a secularized level, into the very totalitarian claim it had led away from during the confessional civil wars."[70]

An illustrative example of this crisis of the liberal state is the *Popetown* case. This is an animated sitcom of British production, originally commissioned by the channel *BBC Three*, broadcast for the first time in June 2005 in New Zealand and never aired in the

69 Cf. P. Sequeri, *Contro gli idoli postmoderni*, p. 88.
70 E.-W. Böckenförde, *The Rise of the State as a Process of Secularization*, in *Religion, Law, and Democracy: Selected Writings*, (Eds.) M. Künkler and T. Stein (Oxford: Oxford University Press, 2021), pp. 152–167, here p. 167.

United Kingdom for the criticism raised. The plot, in fact, sees as its protagonist a fictitious Father Nicholas, who lives in the Vatican City, which refers to the title of the series, and is dedicated to covering the back of the Pope, represented as a *minus habens* capricious and childish. The aim of the protagonist is to prevent the public from discovering the truth about the Pontiff's mental state, disentangling himself from priests with sexual problems, vain nuns and corrupt cardinals, who try to get rich behind the Pope's back. From a quality perspective the series is not noteworthy and has received middling ratings from critics.

The fame of the program is, therefore, mainly due to the controversy raised, since the protest of British Catholics prompted broadcasters to reject the series. As mentioned, New Zealand's channel C4 made a different choice, airing the *sitcom* despite the protests. But the most interesting discussion is the one that concerned Germany, where MTV began broadcasting the episodes in May 2006. The debut was preceded by a commercial aired during Holy Week, that showed Jesus sitting and watching television with the words "laugh instead of hanging around", in the double meaning of loitering around and dangling, with an obvious and disrespectful reference to the crucifixion. The outrage prompted not only the various Christian churches, but also the Jewish and Muslim communities, to ask the network to withdraw the series. In Bavaria, the archbishopric took the matter to court, invoking Article 166 of the German penal code, which deals with the crime of blasphemy.

The judgement of the ninth civil section of the regional court of Munich I, issued on 3 May 2006, deserves to be quoted, because, although legally correct, it highlights a legal paradox, the derivations of which can have considerably dangerous consequences. The article referred to consists of two paragraphs:

(1) *Whoever publicly or by distribution of writings (§ 11 3) insults the content of the religious or ideological confession of others in*

such a way that it disturbs the public peace shall be punished by imprisonment not exceeding three years or a fine.

(2) Similarly, anyone who insults publicly or through the distribution of writings (§ 11, 3) a church or other religious society or ideological association existing in Germany, its institutions or customs, in such a way as to disturb the public peace, shall be punished.

As we can see, the text protects both the content of the religious confession, equated here to any ideological position, and a church or religious society, also equated here to an association whose principle is ideological. But the central point, the reason for the ruling refusing suspension, is that the offenses given must endanger the public peace. The German judges decided that *Popetown* could continue to be broadcast, because the protests did not take on a dimension that would endanger safety, in fact "not every publication that touches the sensibilities of others, no matter how unpleasant or patently inane, is likely to cause concern about harm to the public peace."[71]

In other words, provided that Christians do not respond with violence, their beliefs can be treated without respect. The issue is indeed crucial, in the etymological sense of the term, because the very purpose of law is to give each his own, preventing violence and preserving the common and private good. Here, however, the very opposite is being asserted, because the relationship is not being 'seen'.

The paradox is obvious. All the more delicate the question becomes in a multicultural and multi-religious context such as the one that globalization brings us. Brent Bozell, an American

---

71 ". . . nicht jede Veröffentlichung, die an den Empfindungen anderer rührt, mag sie auch geschmacklos oder schlicht dümmlich sein, eine Beeinträchtigung des öffentlichen Friedens zu besorgen geeignet ist." (ZUM 2006, 579)

conservative writer, in an article in *Townhall*, also in 2006, highlighted the difference between the work of MTV with *Popetown* and the choice of the authors of *South Park*, another satirical television show, not to include the image of Mohammed in an episode.[72] The conclusion is astonishing: The principles of modernity affirm freedom of speech in such a way that only that group whose reaction does raise concern for public peace should be respected, that is, the protection of religious freedom is affirmed only for the violent. Paradoxically, respect for Islam would be due not to its inherent dignity, but to the actions of terrorists. Brent Bozell, in the article cited above, with force and sarcasm, points out that the issue in its depth is not about freedom of opinion, but about economic profit, because Viacom, owner of MTV, does not affirm freedom of expression when there is a loss, but only when it is faced with people whose faith excludes violence. It seems terribly ironic that the cover image of *Popetown* was a caricature of the pope wielding a machine gun. The case shows the action of the idol of communication, which becomes an end in itself, swallowing the audience, like Kronos with his children. Here, in fact, not only is the relational dimension not perceived, but it is even used in a manipulative sense as a means to produce profit.

The depletion of the legacy received from the Judeo-Christian matrix opens up disturbing political perspectives, which the virus has brought to the fore, making it impossible to ignore, particularly because of the role of medical big data and tracking needs. Giorgio Agamben has referred to this situation as biopolitics and thanatopolitics. In *Homo Sacer*, the philosopher writes with extreme lucidity, "This is modern democracy's strength and, at the same time, its inner contradiction: modern democracy does not

---

72   Brent Bozell and Tim Graham, "*South Park*" and "*Popetown*," at Townhall.com, posted April 21, 2006, accessed March 24, 2021.

abolish sacred life but rather shatters it and disseminates it into every individual body, making it into what is at stake in political conflict."[73]

It is still about the modern double-bind that the pandemic sends into crisis by confronting us with the impossible alternative between freedom and health.

Girard's perspective proves important here because it shows the metaphysical role of idols and how there can be no relationship without the transcendent dimension that protects desire from mimetic collapse. Narcissism is not, in fact, a moral problem nor only a psychic one, but a metaphysical one. The success of Christianity tends to be explained in terms of the alliance between religion and politics (e.g. the Roman Empire), but paradoxically the founding principles of Christianity lead instead to avoid such collusion, which instead is always present in the life of the human being, so as to constitute an inescapable philosophical problem, as the condemnation of Socrates narrated in the *Phaedo* indicates. If one tries to eliminate religious discourse from public space, one does not achieve freedom and separation between church and state, but on the contrary falls under the domination of idols as individuals and as a society. Only, you are not even aware of it. Therefore, the real "fall of the wall" that the pandemic makes possible is precisely the overcoming of the post-modern idol of secularization.

Here we are not trying to make a confessional discourse that looks back nostalgically to a certain *ancien régime*, because we are not invoking the Judaeo-Christian matrix as the only possibility of salvation. This reading only points out that the crisis caused by the pandemic can be the opportunity for a relational "conversion" and, if one wishes, but always following the "conversion", also for a relational "revolution", by definition non-dialectical. We need a

---

73 G. Agamben, *Homo Sacer: Sovereign Power and Bare Life* (Palo Alto, CA: Stanford University Press, 1998), p. 103.

form of relational liberalism. This must necessarily start by bringing religious discourse back into the sphere of political and economic debate, because otherwise idols will impose themselves, with their dehumanizing manipulative force.

9. Trinitarian Spirituality

But how can a relational revolution be possible? Isn't this concept contradictory in itself? The answer put forward in this chapter is that such a revolution is possible if we move to a spiritual level, in particular if we open ourselves to Trinitarian spirituality.

We have seen how the pandemic has triggered the perception of a crisis, which has both political and economic dimensions. My proposal is that the roots of this crisis are spiritual and for the same reason theological. I am not merely trying to say: Give money to professional theologians like me because our job is important. For I think that every human being is a theologian, because every human being decides about the meaning of life through his or her practical choices. And this is unavoidable. There is always some sort of theology behind all our existences: Some people know it, others do not. We cannot dodge the issue of the spiritual meaning of our lives.

So this relational revolution is not a question of calling for a political shift to the right or left. From the perspective proposed here, in fact, the two positions are equivalent insofar as they reduce human life to praxis. Obviously the course of action indicated by the different political options would be different, but the convergence would be precisely in identifying the ultimate horizon of choices in action itself. Instead, as we have seen, the human being has an infinite desire, which however inhabits a necessarily finite dimension. This causes the tensions identified by Girard, which make every politician a potential scapegoat, because it is impossible to completely satisfy the (infinite) expectations of people. So, only spirituality can protect man. Indeed, it affirms him as an absolute value in his relationship with a sort of "beyond", from which derives a constant and radical relational openness that avoids conflict. In particular, this is realised in the perspective opened up by the Trinitarian matrix, on the basis of which truth can be presented as relation because God Himself, that is, Being and the foundation of all beings, is in Himself relation. Again in terms of Girard's mimetic desire, in fact, what happens if the attention of (wo)men is directed towards spiritual goods and even more towards relational goods? Obviously the conflict ceases to have any hold, because spiritual realities are not lost when they are communicated, unlike what happens with material goods. In the case of spiritual relational realities, then, the mimetic crisis is radically impossible, because the desired good itself is a relation, that is, it belongs not to one but to all those in relation because it is *between* them and emerges *from* them.

Following Rafael Domingo, a possible definition of spirituality could be "an intentional and experiential union with the universe, humanity, the divine, and, ultimately, the Supreme Being that many people call God."[74] Another option proposed by the same author is "an ontological and transcendent order that links and unites God, the divine, with humanity and the universe in accordance with love."[75] This second definition is even more useful for the present perspective because it highlights the relational dimension that characterises every form of spirituality at a fundamental level. In this sense spirituality is broader than religion, without being dialectically opposed to it, since spirituality is a fundamental element of the very religious phenomenon. According to the

---

74 R. Domingo, "Toward the Spiritualization of Politics," in *Journal of Church and State*, 63(2) (2021), 234–255, here 235.
75 Idem, "Why spirituality matters for law: An explanation," in *Oxford Journal of Law and Religion*, 8(2) (2019), 326–349, here 327.

author quoted, spirituality is descending, while religion is ascending. In other words, the former refers to an original openness and relationality, to which the institutional dimension of the religious phenomenon is a response. This is why spirituality is more universal and holistic, while the latter is more marked by cultural elements and differences.

The question that follows from here is: "What spirituality emerges from the Judaeo-Christian matrix?" Jean Daniélou's approach may prove very valuable in answering this question. The starting point of one of his extremely topical books, significantly titled "Oration as Political Problem", is the recognition of the importance of Emperor Constantine's decision to leave freedom of worship to the citizens of the Roman Empire.[76] The significance of this act for the development of the Christian church in the 4th century would not be linked to fiscal advantages or political favour, hence to an institutional dimension, but deeper, on a spiritual level, the great leap allowed by this decision of the emperor was the possibility of being a Christian even for those who were not strong enough to expose themselves to the risk of persecution. This brought out a fundamental feature of the spirituality linked to the Judaeo-Christian matrix, namely its popular dimension. The very comparison with Gnosticism and pagan traditionalism shows how this element baffled the first Christians' contemporaries. Paradoxically, this option refers back to secularity as a fundamental element of a Trinitarian spirituality. In fact, the word "people" in Greek is *laos*, from which the English "lay" derives. From this perspective, the religious element itself, linked to worship and therefore to a clergy, was conceived in the early church as a service to the people, because Christian spirituality itself was essentially popular. For this reason, it also assumed a political value, in a broad sense.

I would like to share with you an example of this implicit,

---

76 J. Daniélou, *L'oraison, problème politique* (Paris: Cerf, 1965), 12.

everyday spirituality, that is a sort of "pop theology". I was having lunch with a PhD student of mine who is a priest from Los Angeles. Some North Americans were at the table nearby. A couple asked to talk with us. I thought that they were asking for a blessing or putting a question, but they surprised us by saying that they wanted to teach us something that they had learnt from their dad: the "holy high five". Both started moving their right hands and tracing a cross in the air with them, as though blessing each other, but they ended the movement with a high five. It was funny and deep at the same time: What they did can be read as a symbol of the reality that the Trinity is between us, gathers us and keeps us together. Jesus prayed to the Father that we may be one as they are one.[77] Thus, our joy at being together could be expressed through the "holy high five". But it is not just something emotional. There is a deeper spiritual meaning that can be useful for our path. The "holy high five" can be read as a symbol of the truth that my limit is the place where I can be one with you, through the very skin of my hands. Our borders can be bridges which make us free, if we contemplate them in the light of the Trinity and of the Cross. But this works only if we do not hide our differences, but through a spiritual gaze read them as sources of relations. And this time after the pandemic, characterised by the concrete (re-)discovery of our frailty, may be an opportunity to experience this relational revolution.

In fact, as we have seen, if we go back to the Bible, we find the narrative of creation in the book of Genesis. And this can be read as the origin of relational differences. The particular Jewish verb to create – *bara'* – means something like "cutting": It is a separation of light and darkness, of earth and sea, of man and woman. And the human case shows how this division is generative. Adam and Eve have two children, so that through them we can discover

---

77   Cf. John 17:20–26.

that life itself is made of differences: the one between parents and children, the one between brothers, and so on. And in this picture, differences are not only the place but also the source of relations.

The point is that all these differences were lived and read as relations, because in Paradise all differences were relational. Then original sin came into play. If we think of the prohibition to eat the fruit of the tree of life,[78] we can see that the fundamental difference is the one between the Creator and the creatures. The former has given life to the latter. This means that life was not prohibited to the human being. The issue was about the way of obtaining it. Life is a gift and we cannot take it without destroying it. A gift belongs to me but through a relation. It was not mine, and now I possess it because someone else, someone who is different from me, has given it to me, like an engagement ring. So relation is at the very heart of gift giving itself.

As Rafael Domingo notes, from the perspective of the Judaeo-Christian matrix, spirituality is radically defined by the third Person, the Holy Spirit. Therefore, following the thought of Augustine, whose influence on Western culture cannot be stressed enough, the very Spirit must be associated with love, communion and gift. From the perspective proposed here, it is clear that these elements are not only of moral value, but are founded in the ontological depth of reality itself, through the creative act of the triune God. So, according to Trinitarian spirituality, gift is the real and deepest meaning both of life and of the world.

I received a deep impression of this when I was a PhD student in physics and was asked by a visiting Chinese professor, "What is the Trinity?" I was coding at my workstation, and that question came out of the blue as the last thing I could think of. I was taken aback and tried to gain some time by asking about his background. He answered that he was educated in a communist environment

78 Gen 3:3.

and had practically no religious background at all. So I asked if he knew the phenomenon of exchanging presents in China, and, when he answered positively, I explained that a gift requires three elements: the one who makes the gift, the one who receives it and the gift itself. This is one of the best images that we have to approach the mysterious reality that the God of Jesus Christ is triune. In fact, our God is Gift, perfect, absolute and eternal, and so God is one and three at the same time: the Giver, the Receiver and the Gift, given by the Father and eternally and perfectly given back by the Son. Thus, the Spirit is the divine Life itself as mutually donated Gift. In that moment I did not know that this theological approach was Augustine's favourite one, as I later discovered studying theology.

This memory helps me to highlight that differences are both essential and positive, but only when they are relational differences. On the contrary, differences become a problem when we do not approach them as relations. But to avoid this we need the Trinity and a Trinitarian spirituality. And this is very practical and tangible.

In fact, this is what we discover in the Gospel, through the revelation that God is triune, Father, Son and Spirit—Giver, Receiver and the gift of Love. The Jewish people had great difficulty in understanding that God is one, but in the end they got the point after going through deserts and exiles. Then Jesus came and started calling this one God, who is the Creator, with the familiar word "Abba". This sounded crazy to His people. To understand why, we should take into account that, in all Indo-European languages, there are two main roots to express fatherhood: *pater* and *atta*, which correspond to "father" and "dad".[79] There is an essential difference between them: The first implies only origin, while the

---

79 Cf. E. Benveniste, *Le vocabulaire des institutions indo-européennes*, I (Paris: Munit, 1969), pp. 210–211.

second means also identity of nature and belonging to the same family. Bill Gates could be called the "father" of Microsoft, Mao Tse Tung the "father" of the Chinese Nation, I am called "father" by the faithful, but, for the celibacy of the Roman Catholic priests, it would be embarrassing if one of my churchgoers called me "dad". The same applies to the supervisor of a PhD, who in Germany is called *Doktorvater*, i.e. father, but not dad, of the new doctor.

Jesus called God precisely "Dad", not "Father", and was crucified for using such an expression. This clearly meant that He was God. But God is one, so that Jesus is a real human being who, at the same time, is God, because He has and is the same Nature that the Father is. He creates, saves, and raises the dead, as only God can do. But He weeps, is hungry, suffers and dies as a human being. In his humanity, He is forever united to heaven, and time is invincibly connected to eternity, so limitations are revealed as meeting points where infinity is given to us and where inexhaustible life can be poured into us. In Christ we experience again what the Creator was doing. Paul expressed this truth saying that we were created in Him and through Him.[80]

This biblical view puts difference and relation at the basis of our being. In fact, as we have seen, we can be identified with an ontological difference, as we are finite, but our desire is infinite, because we were created in Christ, in the image of God. This is the reason that makes it impossible for any finite reality to fill the desires of our heart. The result is that we always try to go beyond, and that, after the loss of the perfect relation with the Father caused by original sin, the borders become a place of conflict. And this is a serious political issue. Without the Trinity, differences seem dangerous and are so, because we are always trying to conquer anything that is beyond what we already have, overcoming the other. But they are still the place where relations emerge and grow. This

80   Cf. 1 Cor 8:6 and Col 1:15–20.

is why we need Trinitarian spirituality. Through it we can recognise our *limes*, the Latin term which means *boundary* or *limit*, as a *limen*, that is a *threshold* and a *beginning*, a path to a new dimension of reality. In this way, differences can be recognised as sources of wealth, while the denial of differences, as a strategy to overcome the risks of conflict induced by modernity, can reveal itself in all its (dangerous) ineffectiveness.

A joke can help. A woman goes to see her lawyer because she wants to divorce. The latter asks for the reason, and she says that it is the "compatibility" of their characters. The lawyer thinks that he has misunderstood and answers that maybe it is just the contrary, i.e. the "incompatibility" of their characters. Then the lady says that it is exactly compatibility that she means: She likes travelling and her husband likes travelling; she likes sport and her husband does the same; she likes men and her husband likes men...

If we think carefully we can see that business, art, love are based on differences. A price is high if the object is rare, that is, if it is different. A master-work is unique. And love is being one and two at the same time, as it is a relation, i.e. the deepest unity that is founded, paradoxically, on irreducible difference. The Bible shows God's original design where differences were relational, but modernity has denied the Father, forgotten the Source of every gift, and started treating differences as the necessary cause of conflict. This has made differences fearful. The problem before the pandemic was that post-modernity was trying to avoid every conflict by negating differences. In this way, however, the borders multiply. I give a real life example. Earlier we had a classic situation with a boy A who looks at girl B, but the girl's boyfriend, C, becomes angry, so that boy A and boyfriend C fight. Now, as it was reported in the news, girl A is with her boyfriend, B, on a bus when boy C starts looking at boyfriend B. Girl A asks her friends to beat boy C because she thinks that he is gay and is trying something on with her boyfriend. We cannot escape the mimetic desire. This shows how differences cannot be avoided, even more, that their negations create new borders which can potentially cause more problems, without a thought that can recognise them as relations. But to do this we must turn to spirituality, and Trinitarian spirituality in particular. In fact, real freedom is based precisely on spirituality, that is, on the relationship with a greater dimension that can resolve the conflicts that arise from material limitations.

In fact, we cannot be ourselves and accomplish the desire to be unique if we invest everything to follow a pattern, to be similar to a model. Consumerism is damaging to identity. You cannot be yourself buying something that is on sale and produced industrially. This failed attempt causes a dialectical reaction that touches also the political dimension. As Roger Eatwell and Matthew Goodwin explain in their book on national populism,[81] this is not fascism, but develops out of the necessity to defend differences. So it arises in particular under certain conditions, defined in the authors' approach by the 'four Ds': *Distrust* of those governing the country seen as elites unconcerned with the real problems of most people, *Deprivation* at the economic level for the increasing differences, *Destruction* of the ordinary way of life in favor of rapid social changes, *Disalignment* with mainstream political parties. From our perspective, these can be read as the result of the deprivation of the relational content of differences.

In fact, we can accept economic differences if they are relational, that is, if it is possible to do better, to move up the economic scale. Social and economic differences can be perceived as positive if they make the system efficient and protect the weakest. Thus the true ontological depth of economic life too is the relational dimension. Even money is a matter of trust, i.e. it is based on this very

81 R. Eatwell and M. Goodwin, *National Populism: the Revolt Against Liberal Democracy* (Pelican: London, 2018).

dimension. The dialectical opposition of meritocracy and social sensitivity is the result of materialistic and idealistic reductionisms. So some populist parties are voted for because their leaders are perceived as close to people, their language is clear, their feelings are shared. We can complain because we are experiencing a political confrontation made up of slogans and selfies, but the deep reason for what is happening is related to the post-modern negation of differences.

The point is that without relations, we have just idols, tags, ideologies, not persons. As we have seen, we need a little bit of metaphysics here, not in the technical sense. In fact metaphysics is not just a bunch of strange theories developed by a few people in their ivory tower. On the contrary, we use metaphysics every day, as we need it in the kitchen and at the restaurant. Meat is not fish, red wine is not sparkling water. When we choose from the menu, we are closer to Plato and Aristotle than we imagine, as we are making a metaphysical judgement. And when the waitress brings the food, we repeat this, as we check 'what is' on our plate. But this also has biblical roots, since the very moment when Adam was called to name the different animals created by God, without finding anyone to address personally. Then the metaphysical issue was also present in Moses' encounter with the Creator at the burning bush and in the desert with the manna, the name of which - *man hu*[82] i.e. "what is it?" – refers precisely to the fundamental metaphysical question.

So, just as every person is an unconscious theologian, he or she is also a little metaphysician. And we are not just talking about food here, but about the very basis of identity. Because of that, we are highlighting the positive dimension of differences in Trinitarian spirituality. The question is: How do we say that something is this thing and not another or that someone is this one and not another? How do we do it in an increasingly liquid and globalised society?

82   Cf. Ex 16:15.

The Judeo-Christian matrix offers a useful perspective, because it makes it possible to distinguish three basic historical forms of identity:

1. The *tag-like* one, expressed through ideal categories, like those of Plato, Aristotle and Ancient Greece more broadly. This means that you are yourself if you belong to a group, satisfy some conditions, as Aemon should be according to Creon's view. For example, I am a priest, I am a theologian, I am Italian. Obviously this characterisation is helpful, but it does not exhaust my entire identity, in particular it cannot express my uniqueness.

2. The *vs-like* dialectical identity of Hegel and modernity where you are yourself because you are not me. Here being oneself is to be against something or someone else. This means to be through a negation. For example, I am not a layman, I am not a philosopher, I am not Welsh. This form of identity is also useful, because for example it makes it possible to express whether one is married or not, and thus whether one is available for an engagement. But not even this characterisation can express all the uniqueness of the person.

3. Finally, we have the *we-like* relational identity, that is, the Christian and Trinitarian one. You are yourself through and in your relation to the others, as the Father is the Father in the relation to the Son that He eternally fathers and loves in the Holy Spirit. And this does not concern only the Trinity, as the following examples show: I am my father's son, i.e. I am myself through the relation with my father and my father is himself through the relation with me; I am a member of the church, i.e. I am myself through the relations with my brothers in Christ and not just by myself; I am a human being, i.e. I am defined by the relations not only with a category, but with each and all the members of humanity past, present and future.

AFTER PANDEMIC, AFTER MODERNITY

Contrary to the approach of modernity, I cannot be myself alone.

Here it is important to emphasise that the first two forms of identity are eminently logical, while the third requires a shift to the excess of the real. The idea that encouraging conflict between different positions can lead to a better synthesis that eliminates and supplants the contenders is experimentally false, because dialectics always produces more dialectics. The mimetic mechanism only stops when the pain provoked forces one to come out of closure in the mental dimension, as happens with the symptom in psychopathologies. When we enter into conflict, in fact, we do so from the ideal dimension, with which we compare what is in front of us, regardless of whether it is an object or a subject. The glass of water half-full seen by the optimist is there, while the glass of water half-empty does not exist, but is formed in the mind of the pessimist who compares what is there with the idea of perfection that is not there. So identity and dialectics can just be played out in the mind. Instead, the opening of thought to the excess of the real is a simply realist operation, as the half-full glass always speaks of a source. And Trinitarian spirituality favours this, because it constantly highlights the dimension of relational identity.

A terrific example of such a view is offered to us by Ambrose of Milan. It is no coincidence that Augustine, after going through a Manichean and a sceptical phase, converted to Christianity after listening to the sermons of the bishop of the imperial city. In his commentary on the first pages of Genesis devoted to creation, he notes that God did not rest after creating the earth, nor after making the sun, the moon and the stars. Instead, he rested only after creating man. The great Father of the Church explains that this was because from that moment onwards He had someone to forgive. With extraordinary spiritual depth Ambrose reads this as a prophecy of Good Friday, when Christ, who is God, was able to

88

rest after giving all of himself for the remission of human sins.[83] The central point is that the very meaning of the world, the cosmos and history is a relationship stronger than death, namely divine mercy. This vision also has a socio-political value, because from here Ambrose, who had been an imperial official when he was a layman before becoming a bishop, deduces that justice should be identified with mercy.[84] A particularly important moment in Ambrose's life in this regard is the homily during the funeral of Emperor Theodosius (*De obitu Theodosii*), delivered by the bishop on February 25, 395. The relationship between justice and mercy is present at a very deep level in the homily dedicated to such an important believer, who had been readmitted to communion after being excommunicated by Ambrose only five years earlier for ordering the Roman legions to massacre thousands of innocent citizens in Thessalonica, where a revolt against the Goths had broken out.

The line of argumentation is all about gift and gratuitousness as fundamental elements of mankind. Justice, in fact, is mercy and mercy is justice because every human being receives life from others and comes to light in mercy, without which he or she could not subsist and grow.[85] Thus what is most proper to someone, namely life, is of and from another. And this should be kept in mind when we describe justice in terms of "to each his own" (in Latin *unicuique suum*). The deepest and truest identity of the human being is relational. There can be no position further removed from modernity, and the pandemic has made us rediscover the importance of these foundational and gift relationships. This opens up a great opportunity to rediscover, even on a socio-political and economic level,

83 Ambrose, *Exameron* IX, 10, 76.
84 Idem, *Expositio Evangelii secundum Lucam*, II, 90 and *Expositio Psalmi* CXVIII, 23.
85 Idem, *De obitu Theodosii*, 26,7–14: CSEL 73, 384.

the importance of Trinitarian spirituality and the relational identity that derives from it.

This is why Rafael Domingo's proposal to spiritually ground the 'political' triad of the common good, community and government in the Trinitarian root of love, communion and gift is so interesting. Only relational identity, in fact, can protect the 'political' triad from pragmatic reductionism. Instead, common good, community and government are in depth spiritual realities, which are then translated into visible elements. The common good cannot be flattened on the good of the many, neither in a communist nor in a communitarian sense. In fact, if we look at it from the perspective of Trinitarian spirituality, it is simultaneously the good of the individual and the good of the community, because it is the good constituted by the relational identity of each member of society. The common good is the relational good, i.e. the good of the community as a set of relationships, which the government is called to take care of.

The pandemic made us discover how the health of the individual is inseparable from that of the whole community. And this has a metaphysical depth, because from the point of view of the Judaeo-Christian matrix it reveals the relational reality of humanity, which Trinitarian spirituality enables us to see and take care of.

This is why we are living a great opportunity to rethink in a relational sense the different dualisms such as private-public or church-state, which modernity has given us in a dialectical form. It is not a question of eliminating the differences between the two terms in these pairs, but of reinterpreting their identity starting from the relationships that constitute them. The very attempt to protect minorities with dialectics is proving increasingly ineffective. "Me too" or "cancel culture" are not enough to eradicate violence in our societies if we do not develop the capacity to take care of relationships by rereading differences in a relational way.

But this also means that the family must be rethought as a

place where we learn to think in terms of relationships, starting with the fundamental differences between the one and the many, parents and children, man and woman, brother and sister, friends and relatives. As seen in the Greek and Babylonian traditions, the origin of the world was conceived from a fundamental dialectic at this level. Trinitarian spirituality, on the other hand, opens up the possibility of rethinking the family not in a dialectical sense with respect to the rest of society, but relationally. This also has very practical consequences for education, as we shall see in the next chapter.

So my final thesis is that, to overcome this cultural and spiritual crisis caused by modernity and its dialectics, we need to work out post-pandemic the ability to see differences as the place of relations. Christian revelation made this possible, and Trinitarian spirituality does so still.

10. The Vocation of Universities

But how to develop and spread a Trinitarian spirituality? Is this not an idealisation that has little to do with the concrete reality of how the world works, and therefore has no real practical relevance?

The thesis proposed in this final chapter is that universities are the fundamental place where Trinitarian spirituality can and should be developed and nurtured. As absurd as this may sound, it will be attempted to show that universities are either spiritual centres or they are not, for the simple reason that they arose from the Judeo-Christian matrix for this very purpose. I understood this with great clarity in 2005, talking to René Girard at Standford, when he revealed to me that he had decided to move there because the campus was the place that reminded him most of medieval abbeys. The comment puzzled me, but my subsequent studies made me realise that there was something prophetic in the words and choice of this scholar.

But in order to recognise Trinitarian spirituality as the vocation of our universities, it is necessary to start with the purely political question of the foundation of democracy. We all agree in theory that freedom is a fundamental value, but the relational perspective shows us that there is no freedom without a relationship with truth. The pandemic itself and the conflicts that followed it highlighted the need to recognise fake news. The spread of the acronym IRL for 'in real life', which is becoming increasingly popular on social media, cannot avoid reference to the adjective indicating reality. The point is that democracy is not merely a technique of government that works by itself, precisely because it involves the judgement of the people. Once again, it is a question of secularity, in the sense of the Greek *laos*. A democracy is healthier the better its citizens are able to judge. But what does it mean to judge without the reference to truth that some currents in the post-modern era seek to deny? Can there be a democracy after modernity?

The crisis we are experiencing highlights precisely this delicate point, which calls for a relational reassessment of the interaction between the people and the elites. These, in fact, are not an evil in themselves, but are simply results of historical or qualitative differences. If democracy is conceived in purely pragmatic terms as the dialectical negation of all differences and, therefore, of all elites, it ends up going against itself, turning into dictatorship or oligarchy, as the history of the 20th century has shown. Nazism came to power in Germany by democratic means, and the Soviet experience left an oligarchy, suspended between the tension towards a democratic and a mafia-like evolution.

In a nutshell, we need to overcome the (post-modern) dialectic between "the people" and "the elites," because this pair in truth refers to an inevitable difference that we must work to make more and more relational. For example, both communism (the egalitarianism of the collective) and consumerism (the egalitarianism of the individual) did not eliminate elites, but generated materialist (closed) elites, a consequence of their own anti-spiritual approach. In contrast, democracies were born of a spiritual (open) elite. The medieval university itself was characterised by a deeply democratic government. And today, universities are still the place where the future of democracy is played out, because it is here that elites with a spiritual sense can be formed, that is, elites capable of seeing and caring for relationships.

So, the health of a democracy consists in the very relationality of the couple made up of the people and the elite. The latter must know how to take care of the spiritual and relational dimension of society, preventing it from being pervasively manipulated, especially by consumerism and the political use of the media. If the elites are open and meritocratic, because they are able to recognise spirituality as a value, then the whole of society benefits. But where are the elites formed and educated? From where can non-dialectical but spiritual elites arise? Universities must therefore be confronted with their task and vocation. And this is an urgent issue in this post-pandemic time, which requires a real (relational) revolution at the educational level.

In fact, post-modern cultures try to overcome the dialectical tension implicit in the modern approach denying any difference. But, as we have seen, the result of this attempt is the multiplication of differences, that in technical terms is called morphogenesis. In this context, how is it possible to hope to provide to the youth a cultural suitcase that helps them to live if this suitcase is made up only of concepts, models, and information? The archetypes that point to an ideal dimension, which are typical of tradition, and the functionalistic proposals that teach how- to, which are characteristic of modernity, no longer work in such a dynamic context. Much less can a dialectical approach be effective. Any static offering is doomed to be ineffective, because the constant change of context always pushes the text out of play. The surrounding conditions are constantly modified, and the meaning of any proposal gets lost. The enemy against whom one invested this energy is dissolved, and we no longer know where we stand.

In fact, the meaning is given by the relationship between text and context. For example, the term *gift* means "present" in English but "poison" in German. It is the same etymological root that has given rise to opposite meanings, due to the ambivalence of the gift itself in human culture. Think of the Trojan horse, the Greeks' poisoned 'gift' to their enemies. So to understand what the word *gift* means we need to know the context: If it is English it is good, if it is German it is bad. If we receive a package with *gift* written on it, we need to look at the stamp. But in post-modernism the context is always changing, so we have to help reformulate the text so that the relationship between text and context remains the same.

From this perspective, theology has something very practical to offer: The first Christian thinkers found themselves in a similar situation, insofar as in the dialogue with their contemporaries they learned from the Trinitarian matrix and its spiritual content to not *op*-pose principle against principle, but to *pro*-pose the Gospel message showing its relationship with the desire for salvation and fullness inherent in the heart of every human being. The elements of pagan religiosity were scrutinized in order to grasp the good contained in them, i.e. the deeply human dimension they bore, while discarding and purifying them insofar as they were incompatible not with God, but with what is authentically human. From the relational standpoint the disposition of the thinkers of the first centuries of the Christian era was of deep openness on the one hand, and of absolute faith in the fact that the meaning of the creature, of its most authentic reality, is its relation with the Creator. In this way the first Christian thinkers did not imitate the dialectical reaction of their contemporaries, but gradually and despite political persecution, won minds and hearts for God. They carried out what is today called in technical terms a *reframing*. The positive elements of the pagan positions were assumed and inserted into a larger context that, because of its relational strength, illuminated these positive elements even more, showing their beauty and scope. The movement of the text into a broader context, which is revealed as true precisely due to the strength and intensity of the relational dimension that this movement causes to emerge, also seems possible today.

Christian Gnilka is a German philologist who recognised as a defining element of the method of thought of the early Christian thinkers precisely this ability to restore in a larger context elements of truth inherited from their predecessors.[86] The city of Rome is a magnificent representation of this on an artistic and cultural level.

---

86 Cf. Ch. Gnilka, *Die Methode Der Kirchenväter Im Umgang Mit Der Antiken Kultur* (Basel: Schwabe, 1993).

Visiting or even living in it is very instructive, because it shows how this *caput mundi* survived the end of the Roman empire not by its own strength, but by the Christian faith that shaped it as a place that integrated the true and the beautiful regardless of where it came from. It did not dialectically surpass what had preceded it, but relationaly welcomed the positive elements, bringing out a deeper content of which they were bearers. Thus the Roman basilicas are built with beautiful pagan columns and capitals. And this displays a form of thought that spans every Christian era. We have already mentioned the two statues of pagan thinkers on the façade of Como Cathedral. But the examples could be multiplied indefinitely, precisely because it is a method of thinking.

The facade of St Mark's Basilica in Venice is particularly significant in this regard. It is crowned by the statue of the man who was the first evangelist, the patron saint of the city. But this devotion to the patron did not present itself in a dialectical sense in relation to other evangelists. Thus in the 13th century, a magnificent sculptural group of four bronze horses from the Imperial Roman period were brought from Constantinople. These statues, probably belonging to a quadriga located in the hippodrome of the imperial city, were used to express the unity of the four gospels by placing them in the centre of the facade, under the statue of St Mark. The whole thing can be said to crown the very idea of Venice, a city unique for its elegance and beauty, but built in one of the least suitable places, a lagoon with no rock but only sand. In fact, the discovery that tree trunks, completely submerged in mud, did not corrode, but could give stability to the buildings above, allowed this brave city-republic to achieve immense splendor. St Mark's basilica itself is, therefore, built on logs immersed in the mud, like the rest of the city, giving us the magnificent spiritual message that the problem is not our weakness, but the use we make of it. The very wood of the Cross has become the foundation of a way of thinking that has changed the world and will continue to change it. So relational fragility, which is so prevalent in post-modernity, can become a solid foundation for life, for the city, for mankind, if we immerse it in Trinitarian spirituality.

On the contrary, modern reason, due to the loss of a common reference to an exceeding dimension of truth and reality, has become more and more narrow. The various *logoi* no longer allow for communication because they have lost any relational capacity. As we know, their territories are so confined as to no longer overlap. The post-modern subject is thus the slave of a self-absorbed reason that relegates it to ever-smaller regions. Violence inevitably emerges, because dialogue is impossible and the only way of deciding the vital enigmas is to fight. The law of survival of the fittest is imposed without any reference to reason, like between hooligans at a stadium. The interlocutors do not have a common reality to turn to, which is why they cannot turn together toward a single direction, but only collide dialectically to see who wins.

In order to escape from this situation, which inevitably dooms those who are swept up in it to annihilation, an education is needed that allows Christians not to react directly to the denial of their faith and the values that it brings, but that, in the school of the first Christian thinkers, allows for the emphasis of the good in any position and moves the conversation from this to a new framework. For example, the introduction of Halloween in Europe has caused some fears, because it was perceived as a pagan holiday with disturbing dimensions for the desensitization that it induces with respect to the phenomena of death and pain. But a direct opposition to the carnivalesque dimension that appeals to children, who after only a few years are no longer interested in it, does not produce the desired effect. Life is not defended by pitting one principle against another and using models as weapons. Rather, this very occasion can serve to speak of holiness as happiness insofar as it is the vigil of the Feast of All Saints (All Hallows' Eve) and to show that even the most terrible fears can be overcome by gift. To retrieve the positive dimension of paganism, masterfully high-lighted by Daniélou,[87] allows for the repeating of the process that pushed Christians to place the Feast of All Saints precisely in prox-imity with a pagan feast preceding it.

But this process must now be repeated continuously. It cannot be achieved once and for all. This is the illusion that has exposed, in particular since the Middle Ages, Christian culture to modern criticism. The believing thinker—especially the communicator—must constantly resituate the contemporary text into a context that makes the relational value emerge. In a morphogenic society that continues to create differences, such a process must be continu-ously repeated with creativity and courage. However, this requires, on the educational level, a formation for a radical openness to an-other, so that the sharing of common values is not a prerequisite for dialogue. This makes communication possible even in cases where there are maximum differences. In fact, it is precisely relation that can always be revived and recognized among the different el-ements. In this way the constant disposition of seeking relation, accompanied by the "faith" in giving oneself to such an emerging phenomenon, can be the foundation of dialogue.

This has nothing to do with relativism, as the following exam-ple shows. We have certainly heard the story of the blind wise men who tried to guess what an elephant is exclusively by touching it. Each one gave a totally different description from the others, be-cause one touched the leg, another the ear and another the trunk. Each one was right, giving rise to a possible interpretation in a rel-ativistic key, which declares the impossibility of approaching a truth that is not merely sectorial. But it is worth asking what would happen if the blind men were friends and at the same time trusted their tact and their deductions. This would have made it possible

---

87 Cf. Daniélou, *God and the Ways of Knowing*, (San Francisco: Ignatius Press, 2003), 9–43.

to have a non-dialectical or relativistic interpretation of the differences they perceived, transforming them in elements of a single picture, which through relationships would restore a useful and effective outline of the elephant's reality.

Thus today it is urgent to relationally recover the sense of differences, which post-modernity constantly tries to deny for fear of the violence that dialectics can cause. Without differences there are no relationships, which at the same time unite and distinguish. Without differences, there is no beyond, no space for desire. In the example, surprisingly, the awareness of one's own blindness makes the wise blind men open to the other.

Relativism, on the contrary, eliminates the possibility of dialogue itself and creates violence, because there is no other way than dialectic to confront differences. Rather, the repeated experience of the presence of relation, of its flourishing in the desert, of the emergence of something real and true between the interlocutors who are even very distant, favors the onset of this stable disposition, which is analogous to theological faith taken strictly. In the latter, the emergence of relation is given vertically, in the opening of the ontological transcendence of the one and triune God, who seeks man, establishing a covenant with him and who is faithful to the extreme of the Cross. However, given that the Trinity itself is the source of creation, this vertical relation helps one to recognize the emergence of the horizontal relation in the opening of oneself to the other, both as exceeding the dimensions of reality with respect to the 'I' and as a personal difference with respect to the subject. The transcendence of the other thus analogically corresponds with the divine transcendence.

This radical openness to the other, along with a curiosity and deep passion for reality is at the origin of the birth of the university, which were not born by chance in the Christian context. The Judeo-Christian matrix allowed not only for the drive of research in one sector, but for symphonically seeking to recognize all of the relations that exist among the various disciplines, making the various results complete in a single picture that gives glory to God, similarly to what happens with the medieval cathedrals and in the theological *Summae*. This doxological dimension was essential, because it protected reason from mere functionalism. The danger of reductionism still lurks, especially when we move from the stylization of the early Middle Ages to the tendency towards the baroque characterized by later eras. However, the possibility of turning all branches of knowledge in "a single direction" (*uni- versum*) was theologically and spiritually based on the relation between creation, Christ, and the Father. The Son incarnate was recognized as the ultimate meaning of the cosmos, in such a way that the relation between the first two divine Persons and the eternal begetting was placed at the base of the possibility of a "university." The "single direction" (*uni-versitas*) that the researcher could find in reality was given in that reality of being turned to the Father that Christ had revealed in himself. The light of faith allows for the interpretation of the university enterprise in its eminently filial, and therefore relational, dimension. But if the meaning of the world is linked to the Father, this implies that we are all brothers and sisters, and that the world itself is a gift. We must not forget, in fact, that *data* is a Latin term before being English, which university research should help us to reread as *dona*, i.e. in Latin "gifts".

This observation allows one to connect the operation that characterized the cultural work of the Christian thinkers of the first centuries and the medieval project of the university with the current situation of the academic world. First it needs to be noted that the growing demand for the interdisciplinary dimension of research is, in a certain sense, a declaration of the identity crisis into which the university is. In fact, given what has been said, this interdisciplinarity must be intrinsic to the conception of the university itself.

However, the development of the post-modern society undermined the very possibility of a true and proper academic enterprise.

Without the original Judeo-Christian matrix the differences between disciplines cannot be traced to relations that ontologically point to the deepest structure of reality. If we begin to dig from various positions on the surface of a globe toward its center, as we progress deeper the closer we get not only to the center, but also among ourselves, to the extreme of arriving at the same point and independently meeting no matter where we have moved from. This implies that the seriousness of the research leads inevitably to relationship, and therefore to confrontation, with other disciplines and other approaches. However, if we do not know how to treat the differences and thus want to avoid any encounter, then the risk is that voluntarily we are limited to remaining on the surface, to continue to occupy our own space, our own fiercely marked territory like dogs and cats, without wanting to share anything with anyone. But the truest cause of the problem is the attempt to avoid any issue related to meaning and, therefore, the spiritual dimension.

The question we have to ask ourselves, then, is what theological matrix underlies the reality of our universities today. A mental experiment (*Gedankenexperiment*) would be very interesting, even if it could apparently seem a little provocative. Let us compare the conception of society that can be deduced from the experience in today's university faculties with the conceptions presented in chapter three from the Greek and Babylonian traditions, characterized by the "mafia wars" between the gods. This conflict should then be subjected to the critique developed by Plato of traditional myths in the *Euthyphro*. Here he discusses the definition of what is holy. His interlocutor identified it with what is loved by the gods. But this does not hold, because they are constantly fighting each other. In this way, the Greek system of thought asks itself to open up in a spiritual sense, in order to overcome the limits of popular and civil religiosity. Even before the theological matrix, in fact, the classical philosophical matrix had the merit of permitting the development of an academy, as the very origin of the name indicates. The Greek *logos*, in fact, was limited, but open.

This suggests a deep respect for classical philosophical thought, which arose independently of a series of relations in which contemporary thought is immersed. Plato and Aristotle did not in fact know anything about the Trinity. Rather, those who develop atheist or anti-Christian thought today cannot transcend the relations in which they operate. After the revelation of the strength of human desire, and the liberation of the energies of the Judeo-Christian matrix, it is impossible to return to a state of real unconsciousness. Once the emergent effect is produced, reality is definitively changed and can no longer go back. Everyone, in fact, knows through relations, but these relations do not depend only on the subject, but precede it.

Just as we cannot observe the stars with a microscope or cells with a telescope, so we cannot approach what is truly human without addressing the question of meaning and, therefore, without foregrounding the relational dimension. Thus, the modern pretense that epistemological definition should precede phenomenological analysis does not hold. Rather, this very definition is always linked to the phenomenon, that is, to relation.

The crisis of this modern epistemological "priority", in fact, rises from inside the individual sciences themselves, as the theory of complexity reveals. It is not theology that stands as a "school teacher" to discipline the different fields of research, almost in fear that they may say something that does not "sit well." It is, rather, from within the sciences that the phenomenon is produced: Each, according to its own method and its own logic, realizes the insufficiency of a relationally closed approach, like that brought about by the Cartesian matrix.

In fact, scientific research itself has shown the inadequacy of the modern approach. Psychoanalysis is a clear example of the problem: Is it a science or not? Modernity cannot answer as it is obvious that the separation between mind (*res cogitans*) and body (*res extensa*) did not fit in the perspective of a discipline whose very existence was due to the short-circuit between the two dimensions. In fact, a psychopathology affects the body (*res extensa*), without having an immediate cause in it, but in the mind (*res cogitans*).

The example can help to highlight the differences between the Greek *logos*, open to a relational *logos*, and modern reason, which is closed to any beyond, not only supernatural, but also natural. The question is not related to the particular epistemological status of psychoanalysis, because it touches on that core discipline that is logic. With Gödel's theorem, scientific research has come to the conclusion that any logical system so simple as to contain arithmetic cannot be complete, in the sense that, if one tries to deduce all the theorems from the initial axioms, it will not be possible to prove the validity of all of them. In the end the only way to proceed will be to include some of the undecidable theorems among the axioms of the system.[88] This can be translated into the statement that, for the usefulness of any logical system, it is necessary to be open to the reality we are trying to formalize. Somehow, mathematics and physics are not so far from each other. From a theological perspective this result seems coherent, because in the 4th century, Gregory of Nyssa[89] and Gregory of Nazianzus,[90] in order to explain the methodological coherence of thought that proceeds not only from cosmic data but also from that offered by revelation, developed a strategy parallel to the one used now to demonstrate

---

88 See in this respect the first part of A. Driessen – A. Suarez (eds.), *Mathematical Undecidability, Quantum Nonlocality and the Question of the Existence of God* (Dordrecht -Boston: Springer, 1997), 3–56.

89 Cf. Gregory of Nyssa, *De vita Moysis*, II, 235–236: SCh 1, 107–108.

90 Cf. Gregory of Nazianzus, *Oratio 29* (*De Filio*) 9:17–22: SC 250, 194.

Gödel's theorem.[91] On the contrary, this result from the field of logic undermines the positivism and determinism that have characterised the epistemological approach of modernity. They had their zenith with Pierre-Simon Laplace, who asserted with certainty that an intelligence so vast as to know all the positions of all objects in the cosmos and so powerful as to be able to elaborate this information could know both the past and future development of the universe.[92]

This vision entered into crisis within science itself, when Henri Poincaré showed that the possibility of conceiving nature as a book written in numbers is limited. In fact, it is not possible to know with infinite precision the initial conditions of the objects present in the universe for the simple fact that the instruments of analysis are limited. Moreover, there are discontinuities in matter, which is not continuous, but discrete, and above all it is always in motion, even if this is minimal. These elements are essential when working with complex systems, in which any small inaccuracy in the initial information is transferred exponentially in the dynamics of the system. In practice, reality is made up of complex systems and therefore their development cannot be foreseen in a deterministic way, but only on the basis of probability calculations.[93]

One consequence of all this is known as the "butterfly theorem", according to an effective metaphor elaborated by Edward Lorenz in 1972. In his numerical computations on theoretical models for weather forecasts, by pure chance, he realized that the results changed completely if the calculations were repeated with little change in the accuracy of the initial data. For example, if the model

91 Cf. G.J. Chaitin, *The Unknowable* (New York: Springer, 1999), 18–19.
92 Cf. P. Laplace, *Essai philosophique sur les probabilités* (Paris: Bachelier, 1840), 4.
93 Cf. H. Poincaré, *Science et méthode* (Paris: Ernest Flammarion, 1920), 68–69.

forecasts were re-computed with initial conditions that were one part in a million different from the previous ones, the result could be as different as he was between good weather and a tornado. From there came the title of the lecture he gave to the *American Academy for the Advancement of Science*, in which he wondered whether the flapping of a butterfly in Brazil could cause a tornado in Texas.[94] From here developed the research on the phenomenon of chaos, which is present in very different fields, such as biology and finance.

From a theological-philosophical perspective it is important to clarify that the butterfly itself does not cause the tornado, but that human ability to foresee would have to take into account something as insignificant as the movement of the air caused by the wings of a butterfly in Brazil to distinguish between good weather or a tornado in the weather in Texas.

It is as if in nature itself there were a limitation to human knowledge that is not due to the finite capacities of the subject, but is intrinsic to the very nature of the objects studied. This became even clearer with the discovery of quantum mechanics, where it has been shown that it is not possible to think of particles of matter as small planets, because an electron has effects that correspond both to atom-like realities and to waves. In fact, if electrons are fired against a sheet with two slits, they manifest an interference phenomenon, which occurs only for waves, and do not give a result comparable to what would be obtained by throwing stones through the slits. This required that a double nature be postulated for matter: corpuscular and wave. The consequence of this discovery was the impossibility of determining with infinite precision both the position and velocity of particles at the quantum level.[95]

---

94 Cf. E. Lorenz, *The Essence Of Chaos* (Seattle: University of Washington Press, 1995), 181–184.

95 Cf. R.P. Feynman, *The Feynman Lectures on Physics*, I (New York: Basic Books, 2011), 2,6–11.

In this context, it is important to observe that there appears to be a cognitive limitation intrinsic to nature itself as when one investigates a system that presents chaos in a dimension where the effects of quantum mechanics are relevant, one can notice how the chaos disappears just when quantum undecidability appears.[96] It seems, therefore, that physical reality eludes a representation that encloses it, and instead always refers back to a surplus.

It is clear that this complexity, which is linked to the relational depth of the various disciplines, can only be grasped when one moves within a unitary perspective, which does not absolutize the differences between the various areas of knowledge, but rather approaches them in a way that is not only inter-disciplinary, but also trans-disciplinary, i.e. a type of research that involves different disciplines in the search for a holistic view of reality.

But are our universities designed to move with this breadth or do they keep us locked in a Cartesian epistemological "hell"? Returning to the provocative parallelism just proposed between the society of the pagan gods, mafia, and our academic world, a concise formula that I heard during a visit to the USA can be (provocatively) useful: I was told through a joke that the major universities start out as academies, gradually become businesses, and risk ending up rackets.

This clearly is a *boutade*, but at the same time such judgment, certainly the result of a generalization, may suggest a question that guides research: How human are our universities? How human and how humanizing? And do they foster spirituality? Does teaching introduce the students to the complexity of reality in a truly open way? Inevitably, these questions run parallel to that about the

96   Cf. G.Casati, G.Maspero and D.Shepeliansky, "Quantum fractal eigenstates," in *Physica D: Nonlinear Phenomena*, 131 (1–4) (1999), 311–316.

society in which we live, with the dehumanization from which it suffers precisely due to the lack of relationality.

However, this parallel allows us to note that society is the result of the university that preceded it. The most glaring example are the societies produced by the Nazi and communist ideologies with respect to the universitary venture of Georg Wilhelm Friedrich Hegel, with a link to a certain secularised theological matrix that animated it. And so also it is evident to everyone today the relevance of the thought of Clive Staples Lewis or Gilbert Keith Chesterton, that is due to the very fact that their thought was developed in an academic context which anticipated the social pathologies that we live today. In this sense these authors, with their radical Christianity, could serve an extremely interesting function in indicating a path for returning to an authentic university life.

What has been said in this last chapter highlights the valuable and indispensable role of a field of study which, from within the current university institutions, takes on the spiritual dimension and the search for meaning. This can take different forms, both scientifically and institutionally, depending on the context (presence of theology in *curricula*, programs in Christian Humanism, Catholic Studies or Christian Culture), but this task is vital and urgent, if the academic world is to continue to perform its role of service to humanity.

We cannot, in fact, underestimate the extremely practical and concrete value of university research and teaching on the basis of a functionalist claim, due to the disruptive strength of ideas and the generativity that characterizes them. The question therefore focuses on this generative relation and on how it works. Jesus said "by their fruit you will recognize them",[97] that is, by the relation that is at the principle of each thing and that is at the principle of the University and of any form of knowledge.

97   Cf. Matt 7:16.

This is confirmed by the very names that indicate the top educational level in the different ages, from antiquity to modernity, or at least that identify different intellectual ventures that from our standpoint, however, appear as historically and relationally connected. In fact, the *Akadêmia* was a farm about six stadia (a little more than one thousand yards or meters) from Athens where Plato taught. It takes its name from *Akadêmos*, an Athenian hero buried there in a grove of olive trees.[98] It was here that the great philosopher had founded his school upon his return from Italy around 387–388 BC. The choice seems significant in light of some information offered by the myth of the hero figure: The latter had saved Athens from the wrath of the Dioscuri, Castor and Pollux, who were angered by the kidnapping of their sister Helen, who was in that moment twelve years old and who would later, due to her beauty, be the reason for war with Troy when she was kidnapped by Theseus, king of the city. *Akadêmos* revealed the place where the girl was kept hidden, thus saving the city from a fight with formidable opponents. The etymology of the name signifies, according to some reconstructions, "one who is far from the common people." The traits of the myth seem well-adapted to the intention of the platonic philosophical venture that seeks to save the *polis* by indicating a road that protects from violence through an open *logos* that goes beyond *doxa*, that is, beyond common opinion.

The theological origins of the *Universitas* have already been seen, which allow for a reinterpretation of all reality from the perspective of a single direction (*uni-versum*) that now not only is beyond the opinion of the many, but is radically beyond the cosmos. The *logos* in Christ is open, in fact, not only to finite being, but to the infinite source of all things who is the Father. He is the

---

98 Cf. Carla M. Antonaccio, *An Archaeology of Ancestors: Tomb Cult and Hero Cult in Early Greece* (Lanhan: Rowman & Littlefield, 1995), 187–189.

relational term of the single "direction" (*uni-versum*) toward which all is turned.

Very *di*-verse (*di-versum*), that is, directed elsewhere, is what happens with the encyclopaedia (*Encyclopédie*) of the Enlightenment, which according to its etymology turns the formation (*paedeia*) back in a circle (*en-cyclo*). With respect to the project of integral research of antiquity, we now have a semantic passage from formation to information, which tries to fix knowledge, eliminating the very possibility of an ontological *other* and, therefore, denies any exceeding dimension that is not merely formal.

This inverts the process of unfolding the Greek *logos*, made possible by the Judeo-Christian theological matrix, which frees the desire of man and allows him to interpret the whole human depth of the universe. The health crisis with its consequences, however, has brought out strongly the vocation of universities as a service to the human being's search for spirituality and meaning. In fact, just as the liberal state comes into conflict with its own principles if it detaches itself from the Judaeo-Christian matrix that generated it, the same happens to the university. Closure to the spiritual surplus causes an illogical contradiction, as Gödel's theorem itself demonstrates, if one dares to relate the different disciplines, as the very essence of the university enterprise requires.

11. Conclusion: A Call

The health crisis linked to Covid-19 is not only a singular circumstance that can favor the recovery of a relational dimension of human life, previously supported by the Judeo-Christian matrix. Instead, a picture is being drawn in which pandemics will be recurrent, with a ten-year cadence. This practically coincides with what happens in the economic sphere. Benoît Mandelbrot, a Polish-Jewish physicist transplanted in the USA, has analyzed this field from the point of view of the science of complexity, reaching the conclusion that we mistakenly expect a linear market.[99] But with the current organization it is, instead, "chaotic" in the technical sense. With a metaphor we could say that if we find a crevasse in the middle of a city, we should be surprised and the event is news, but if we walk on a glacier it is natural to find, one after the other, a series of crevasses. Here, according to Mandelbrot, our economic system is not a city, but a glacier, that is, the place at high altitude most similar to a desert.

This synchronicity allows us to say that both economic, political and health crises seem to be already the result of that loss of relationality that is the critical element of this discussion. For this reason, we cannot ignore the message of the pandemic and what came after it, we cannot turn a deaf ear to the question it poses. We should keep in mind that psychoanalysis has taught us that when faced with trauma that is difficult to process, the unconscious

99   Cf. B. Mandelbrot, *The (mis)behaviour of markets: a fractal view of risk, ruin and reward* (London: Profile books, 2010).

defends itself by trying to absorb the memory through the process of removal. What other disguise will the idols assume in post-modernity, reinforcing the double-bind chain? What other mask will cover their true face? Ecological consciousness, which the pandemic will rightly reinforce, could turn against the human being, as it already does in some forms of extreme ecologism. Increased computer and IT literacy brings with it the risk of a further retreat of authentically personal communication, because of the substitutive role that the new tools can assume. The weakening of the economic system could relaunch the utopia of a world that eliminates poverty by structurally suppressing differences and, therefore, the real possibility of growth. But the "grace" is that now the crisis itself indicates the relationship as a way out of the impasse that already characterized the Western world, marked by the crisis of modernity. And this must be done together, precisely because what is at stake is relational. So it is necessary to respond to the call for a new culture and a new post-modern economic-political approach that puts the care of real relationships at the center.

It is about rediscovering the value of the limit as a gift that reveals the infinite depth of the human heart. And the task is urgent, because when idols fall, new ones always arise, or rather, the same ones soon return in new guises. Therefore, we must hurry to reread Nietzsche's will to power (*Willen zur Macht*) and Freud's pleasure principle (*Willen zur Lust*), characteristic of modernity, or Foucault's will to know (*volonté de savoir*), the mark of post-modernity, as simple, partial and reductive concretizations of that will to meaning (*Willen zum Sinn*), which according to Viktor Frankl characterizes the human being. And in light of the proposed path, we can say that the pandemic reveals the will to meaning in the human being as a deep desire for relationship (*Willen zur Beziehung*).[100] In fact, the simple bond of

---

100 The expression literally appears in the psychoanalytical thought of the tormented Otto Gross, in contrast to the sexual reductionism of

religo also applies to the herd, as a reference to a necessary and limited dimension, while the true human relationship is given in the approach of *religo* (binding) to the *refero* (referring), which, while remaining in the finite, refers to the infinite and, therefore, opens thought to difference and the encounter with the other. We owe it to ourselves, to our children and, also, to those who have gone before us, because this is the message that Aemon, Antigone's fiancé, is waiting for. From the most sublime depths at the onset of human culture he continues to respond to his father Creon, who again and again upholds the inexorability of the law to defend the *polis*, accusing Oedipus' daughter of being infected with the "disease" of rebellion, because with her loyalty to the family she endangers the city:

Cr.   And is she not infected by this disease?

Em.   The whole people of Thebes deny it.

Cr.   Will the city then suggest to me what orders I should give?

Em.   Do you see? You are the one who speaks like a boy.

Cr.   And so I should govern this country to please someone else?

Em.   No city belongs to one man.

Cr.   But is it not customary to say that a city belongs to the one who rules it?

Em.   You should reign in a desert.[101]

Here Greek humanism bequeaths to us the diagnosis of the impossibility of founding the city on law alone. We need to refer

Freud's approach, and in the works of the philosopher Franz Rosenzweig, from whom it passes to Martin Buber. Here the formula is re-proposed not only in a psychological and sociological key, but even before that as a metaphysical-ontological element that founds the human being.

101 Sophocles, *Antigone*, 730–739.

to something beyond, to the relationships that constitute the people, to the family. It takes openness to escape the tragic knot that the gods inexorably tighten. The clash with the limit in the desert of the pandemic can be a frustration that we can culturally configure as a collective initiation that allows us to open up to a rebirth that, for those who believe, already smacks of resurrection. Perhaps the words of Romano Guardini, taken from his last letter from Lake Como, can seal this heartfelt appeal to work together, to enter together, as human beings and brothers, into the post-modern era. At the conclusion of a series of eight letters in which the reader can feel the philosopher's acute pain in the face of the perception of the loss of balance, due to the advance of technology, in that synthesis between the human being and nature that had configured the landscapes in which he was immersed, the depressive tones are replaced by a message of profound hope, anchored in the awareness that technology itself has been made possible by that Judaeo-Christian matrix mentioned here:

> We must not oppose what is new and try to preserve a beautiful world that is inevitably perishing. Nor should we try to build a new world of the creative imagination that will show none of the damage of what is actually evolving. Rather, we must transform what is coming to be. But we can do this only if we honestly say yes to it and yet with incorruptible hearts remain aware of all that is destructive and nonhuman in it.[102]

These indications of Romano Guardini confirm the line of development proposed in the path presented here. In order to carry out this relational revolution, capable of leading post- modernism

102 R. Guardini, *Letters from Lake Como: Explorations in Technology and the Human Race* (Grand Rapids, MI: Eerdmans, 1994), pp. 80–81.

beyond the shoals of a post-human and post-truthful conception, we need spirituality. And the Judeo-Christian matrix naturally provides a Trinitarian spirituality that frees us from the idealistic antithesis between identity and dialectics, to refer to the excess of a real third. This implies care at all levels from the socio-political to the familial, of the relational gaze, that is, of an ability to read the relationship in the fabric of the real. But in order to accomplish this task, universities must shun a purely functionalist function, which debases their identity. Without in any way detracting from the need to learn a trade and prepare serious professionals for the labour market, what cannot be allowed to happen is that this process should take place to the detriment of the search for meaning and, therefore, to the detriment of the humanity of the young people of today and tomorrow.

Chesterton, with his profound critical humor, offered us what is perhaps one of the most acute representations of the dramatic knot in which our universities find themselves in relation to their vocation as spiritual drivers. In *Manalive*, a novel conceived in 1900, right at the turn of the new century, the protagonist Innocent Smith[103] is crazy in the eyes of both common sense and scientific theory, as he always enters his house like a thief in order to possess it for real, and he continually conquers again his own wife. He states, in fact, that "When you're really shipwrecked, you do really find what you want."[104] And, on the model of the Three Wise Men who found home in Bethlehem following the star,[105] he understands the revolution as a return.[106] So he shows up at night, armed with a gun, for a real philosophical and academic "duel"

103 Cf. G.K. Chesterton, *Manalive* (New York, John Lane, 1912), 169–175.
104 *Ibid.* 58.
105 Cf. 264.
106 Cf. 245.

with Emerson Eames, Warden of Brakespeare College in Cambridge. He is a scholar and follower of Arthur Schopenhauer, profoundly marked by his existential pessimism linked to the affirmation of the presumed death of God. So he teaches that life is not worth living and that suicide would be the most rational solution. Then Innocent Smith threatens him with death to test the professor's theory. When this professor asks to live, as dawn breaks, the protagonist reveals that he himself was risking death, because he risked the death penalty if the truth about the meaning of life did not win in the confrontation with the Warden.[107] In this way, the truth of their thought was put to the test by forcing the openness of theory to confront reality, which here, dramatically, is death, the ultimate limit.

The real philosophical duel between Innocent Smith and poor Emerson Eames starts from a mystical and metaphysical position: The real reality is *beyond,* and thought seeks it through reflection. The point is that this position is perverted by pessimism, which folds back on itself instead of reading this structure of thought in the light of relation as a sign of the presence of the source of desire for infinity, which attracts to that *beyond.*[108]

Everything is suspended between the two verbs *will* and *wilt.* In order for there to be a future, desire is needed, but it must always challenge the limit that is constantly emerging as evidence, despite the promises of technology and the narratives in which we are immersed. Facing the possibility of wilting leads to the possibility of willing. The health crisis and its aftermath represent a change of epoch, accelerating the end of modernity and leading us definitively into post-modernity. The challenge is what the latter will look like. What is said here presents the need for a relational revolution that can only come about as a spiritual revolution. The

---

107 Cf. *ibid.* 178.
108 Cf. *ibid.* 162.

modern narrative that religion is the cause of the dialectic afflicting humanity clashes with the evidence that spiritual and relational goods are not lost in being given away, unlike material goods. Thus, faced with the promise of globalisation, financialisation and the consumerist approach to society now common to every political translation, the pandemic has played the role of judgement, as in Innocent Smith's "duel".

And this also has a profound meaning for our democracies. The point is that liberalism depends on the conception of freedom to which it refers. If freedom is freedom to consume, then any difference between left and right falls away, because what unites is only praxis, no matter whether the banking function is centralised by a single party or an association of states.

At the heart of the question of freedom, which leads to the migratory flows to Europe and the USA, i.e. a sort of "foot voting," is the relationship. Indeed, one is free when one can be in relationship with others. For example, poverty and crime greatly limit such freedom. Thus the migratory flow back from South America to Europe is often dictated by the limitations imposed on freedom not by an oppressive government, but by the crisis of relationships induced by the poverty-crime combination.

The problem is that consumerism, now absolutely transversal in all forms of government, has begun to consume relationships. The process began with the irruption of the market in the intimate and generative relationships between men and women, to reach a form of paroxysm with social media, where the product itself is not substances but relationships and the language with which we communicate, goods that are by definition private and common at the same time. Hence the great opportunity to see and care for relationships, to which those who have the responsibility of educating future generations are called in the first place. Work itself can, in fact, change meaning if it is not reduced to a mere effort to earn what can then be later used to consume. Indeed, if relationships are the deepest fabric of reality, as creation reveals according to the Judeo-Christian matrix, then the possibility of a spirituality that unites work itself with care for others, especially one's own family and the weakest, is opened up. Thus the daily life of each person can be transfigured by and in relationships, giving a real answer to that sense of the infinite that dwells in the heart of every human being.

The very cover of this volume, with its lightness, is intended to illustrate the relationality that underlies our lives, even the most everyday one, as that of the family. But these relationships are the fruit of an ontological "inner link" with a greater dimension that draws us towards heaven from within our hearts. The challenge that post-modernism should not be a dialectical negation of the human being systematically implemented in the name of overcoming the question of truth passes precisely through this relational revolution, which can begin simultaneously in universities and families, and then be invested in every aspect of human life.

In fact, eliminating the Judeo-Christian matrix runs the serious risk of losing relational thought. But pandemic means that what hangs as a threat on (*epi*) the people (*demos*), i.e. epidemic, has now become a matter of the whole (*pan*) people, i.e. pandemic, so that, as in the desert, there is no possibility of evading the question of what lies before us, of what constitutes us as persons. But it is precisely Trinitarian spirituality that can offer an answer capable of triggering the relational revolution that we urgently need in order to continue being human.